From victim To Victory

From victim To Victory

Meghan Huston

XULON PRESS

Xulon Press
2301 Lucien Way #415
Maitland, FL 32751
407.339.4217
www.xulonpress.com

Book edited by Marla Black & Maia Mastoridis

The events and conversations in this book have been set down to the best of the author's ability, although some names have been changed to protect the privacy of individuals.

Paperback ISBN-13: 978-1-6628-1134-0

Ebook ISBN-13: 978-1-6628-1135-7

FROM VICTIM TO VICTORY

20 20

To all of the victims/survivors out there:
This story is for you.
You are not alone. You are loved. You are worthy.
You have a voice no matter who told you that you don't.
Your voice deserves to be heard.
You are not a piece of property.
It's okay to tell.

*To my family, my friends, and my wonderful
treatment team(s):*
Thank you for believing in me.
Thank you for sticking by my side through both the dark
times and the light.
Thank you for your continuous encouragement and support.
I wouldn't be here today without you guys.
I love you all.

contents

author's note.

I know what it's like to go through life thinking
you're not worth anything. Like your only purpose in life is to
suffer. I know what it's like to want to continue the punishment for yourself because it's comfortable...because it's the
only thing you know. I know what it's like to give everything
to other people to make them happy and have nothing left for
yourself. I know what it's like to think that getting help feels
like the end of the world in the moment but then realize it is
the start of the life you've always deserved.

 Throughout my recovery journey and healing from my
abuse, I have found my voice. I have found my worth. I have
found the little girl inside of me.

 This story is raw. It is written from both the eyes of the little
girl within me and through the eyes of the older/wiser version
of myself. Some of the writings are taken from my journal(s)
that I wrote while I was in treatment working through trauma
and my eating disorder. I am a very visual person and my brain
has worked through the trauma (and is still healing) in a very
unique way. I am excited to share my journey with you!

 Sorry not sorry to all the english majors out there who will
get annoyed with the fact that some things are in lowercase

letters—there is a purpose for that. While finding my inner child, I am letting her tell this story. I am letting her use her voice that she has spent her whole life thinking she had none. I am letting her show everyone her world though her little, innocent, eyes. She is not hiding anymore. The lowercase represents the victimization I experienced.

Your brokenness is welcome here.

PROLOGUE:
to the little girl.

to the little girl.
to the little girl who ran and hid because fear was
chasing her.
to the little girl whose innocence was taken at three and
then again for the rest of her childhood.
to the little girl who ran and hid because her reality was a
nightmare—one she could not wake up from.
to the little girl who didn't have a voice.
to the little girl who was told she had to be perfect in order
to be loved.
to the little girl who had to go numb to survive.
to the little girl who feels worthless.
to the little girl who feels like she must continue to hide in
order to be safe.
hello?
If you can hear me, you can come out now.
It's safe.
I'm here to protect you and give you the life you've
always deserved.
-Megs

CHAPTER ONE:

when innocence was lost.

the day my innocence was taken was the day i was forced to grow up.

People have asked me if I were to go through every-thing that I went through again, would I change anything? My response is always, "No. No i would not change a thing." Some people are shocked, some people understand, others do not understand at all. You see, everything I have gone through has made me into the person I am today. Believe it or not—I am starting to like her. Liking myself is still something I am working on but I have made a lot of progress. It took a lot of tough work for me to be able to look into the mirror and tell myself, "I am a human being who deserves to be happy. Who deserves to eat. Who deserves to take up space in this world. Who is worthy of love and to be cared for." I have learned it is normal to have two feelings at once and they are allowed to be completely opposite. Weird, I know.

Throughout this book, I am inviting you into my life. Throughout this journey, if you need to take time for your-self—do it. You deserve it. I am giving you written permission to do so if you are someone who needs permission to do things like I once was.

i don't really know where to start. *insert laugh that's triggered by anxiety.*

on may 27 in sarasota, florida; my mom and dad are welcoming a baby girl into the world. my mom is ecstatic and my dad fell in love instantly. from the day i am born, my dad is wrapped around my tiny innocent fingers. as i grow, my mom shares with me she was afraid to have a girl...i think i know why now. i am the oldest of three—my brudder is the middle and my sister, the youngest. my family attends church every sunday morning. in fact, we are very involved in the church. my dad is in charge of the sound and my mom in charge of the power points. both of my paternal grandparents are also very involved in the church. everybody knows us pretty well...at least they think they do. no one actually knows what is truly happening behind closed doors. no one knows the numbness i feel. the fear that is always lingering in the back of my mind. the anxiety that feels like i can't breathe. the hate i have towards me. people at church sometimes asks me why i am crying when they see me. of course, i quickly reply with "i'm not" which is obviously a lie. i wonder what would happened if i do tell someone what is happening to me? would someone believe me? would it actually stop? am i going to get in trouble?

no. i can't. i can't betray my dad like that. i promised him.

my dad is overly nice to people. he jokes around, is the life of the party, knows what to say at the right moments, and is very respected by everyone around him. it is like some people fear him. do they have a reason to? i mean, i think so… but no one else even knows what he is doing. everyone loves him. maybe everyone loves him because along with all the positive things about my dad, he is also very manipulative. he manipulates me and everyone around him.

some days i still wonder how he gets away with what he does.

somethings i will never know or understand. i believe my life is normal. it is all i know. how am i supposed to know dads are not supposed to have sex with their daughters?

the first time i am touched i am two years old. i become a doll being used for other people's pleasure at two years old. my body becomes unsafe and unlovable at two years old. my body becomes property at two years old. my body is not mine.
i don't know what is happening to me. i feel dirty. i don't know what is happening to me but it doesn't feel right. i don't know what is wrong but something is. "i'm sorry" becomes the most natural phrase that flows from my mouth. when i get hit, the "i'm sorry's" become more frequent. i'm sorry for being bad. i'm sorry for making a mess. i'm sorry.

confusion.
i'm confused.
confused as to why this is happening to me. what do you mean it isn't normal to get hit and raped all the time? what is a childhood supposed to consist of?
while growing up being manipulated, i learned at a young age that if i wanted something, i just had to "do a favor" to get it.

my dad starts out with touching me inappropriately and "playing around." it is our little game, he explains to me. i feel special. it is our secret…the two of us…i grew to love secrets.

"i have to pee."
"no, you don't it just feels like you do."
"no i really gotta go."
dad starts beating me because i am not being cooperative.
why would anyone want to feel like they have to pee but don't really have to go? it doesn't make any sense. after a while the touching turns into dad having sex with me. the first time it happens i am home sick from school and the only thoughts going through my brain are, "why is he doing this to a sick girl?" and "please make it stop. it hurts." at that point a piece of me, the little girl inside of me, went and hid. she is terrified. she is hurt. she is lonely. she is lost. i mastered the skill of disassociating. "abcdefghijklmnopqrstuvwxyz now i know my abc's next time won't you sing with me? abcdefghijklmnopqrstuvwxyz now i know my abc's next time won't you sing with me?…" i sing the alphabet to "go away" so i don't feel the pain because it is all i know how to do in the moment. i learn pretty quickly that screaming, kicking, crying, and hitting isn't going to make the bad things stop. it only make them worse. so in a way, the alphabet saves me. if i don't want to feel something, i sing my abc's.

why is dad nice and then mean? does he even care about me? dad says he loves me, but it doesn't feel that way. there has to be something wrong with me. i have so many misconceptions about love and what a family is supposed to look like. i'm so confused. the most confusing part of it all is that i still love my dad. there are still good times in my life even though i don't remember them…i can feel them.

when dad has sex with me or beats me, afterwards he will say "i'm so sorry." sometimes i am mad at him but the majority of the time i just tell him "it's ok" because i don't want to make him feel bad. i feel sorry for him.

why can't i just be a good daughter?

why do i have to keep messing up?

if i just listen better, he won't get so mad at me.

i don't deserve to be alive.

dad puts me down. he tears my confidence to pieces and makes me truly believe i am worth nothing…that i am less than garbage. that i am just a worthless piece of property. that i am too fat, too ugly, and too annoying. i hate me. i don't have any self-worth. i don't deserve to. my innocence is stolen. it was taken by someone who should have loved and protected me. who should have taught me how to respect my body and love myself. who should have taught me how boys were <u>supposed</u> to treat me. who encouraged me and told me lame dad jokes.

the day my innocence was taken was the day i was forced to grow up.

Journal prompt:

Write a letter to your younger self.

_____

_____

_____

_____

_____

_____

_____

_____

_____

_____

_____

_____

_____

_____

_____

_____

_____

CHAPTER TWO:

property.

i wish i could say that once i got older the abuse
stopped...but if i did, i'd be lying to you...

i am about six years old now. i feel like property and like
my only purpose in this life is to suffer.

one day dad got his photography equipment out and set
everything up. he put up the backdrops he had and the lights.
dad got his camera out and told me to stand in front of the
grayish blue marbled backdrop. i did what i was told. *snap*
snap *snap* dad is testing his camera. i'm wearing a sundress
and holding my teddy bear. *snap* dad takes more pictures.
"come on, smile." i smile. i do what i am told.

dad told me to take my clothes off. tears rolled down my
face "i don't want to." dad got mad. i don't like it when dad
gets mad...he gets mean. where is mom? where is my brudder
and sister? why am i always alone with dad? "you better get
your clothes off or else." i don't know why dad always says "or
else" because he does what he wants to do to me anyway. i take
my clothes off and stand there in the middle of his backdrop.
naked. dad poses me. *snap* *snap* *snap* the pictures continue. "you're doing a good job, baby." i get rewarded. dad

tells me we'll go pick out a toy from walmart if i am good and finish the photoshoot.

i saw the red light come on and dad starts walking away from his camera towards me. it's now on video. i know what is coming next. i start crying and telling him "no no no please." i should've known that was not going to stop him. he does what he wants. i lay there.

abcdefghijklmnopqrstuvwxyz now i know my abc's next time won't you sing with me. abcdefghijklmnopqrstuvwxyz...

the alphabet plays in my head over and over again until i become numb and can no longer feel anything. i can't feel my dad raping me. i can't even feel him breathing. i am completely numb and not present. i know how to escape. dad doesn't realize i do this, but it is the only thing i know how to do. i learned kicking and screaming doesn't work. i escape in my mind. the mind is a powerful place.

the "photoshoot" gets done and we go to walmart. i pick out a stuffed animal to go with my other ones. i don't play with them. i keep them in a laundry basket. they are my trophies for being good. it shows me i am not bad. sometimes i will let my brudder and sister play with them but then i get jealous. i earned them.

somedays dad tells me to sit on his lap by his computer and we would watch other dad's do what my dad does to me. dad tricked my brain and made me think it was okay for dads to be having sex with their kids. it's not. i thought all dads did what my dad does to me.

this is my normal.

it felt weird when the abuse wasn't happening. sometimes my dad was a good guy. sometimes we have family nights and get pizza and play games or watch movies. those nights are fun. my favorite game is playing just dance on the wii. sometimes during movies though my dad would force himself inside of me. mom told me no one is supposed to touch me there, but dad said it was okay. that always confused me. i didn't tell mom what dad was doing though. dad said she would get mad.

my favorite times are when dad lets me eat without calling me names. he calls me fat and a disgusting pig sometimes. he usually does that when i eat more than i was supposed to. dad showed me the amount i was allowed to have but sometimes i would sneak more. it was only bad when i would get caught because i would get in trouble for not listening to him. i was just hungry. sometimes when i ate what i was "supposed to" for a while, i wouldn't feel hungry anymore. it was like eating was bad. dad comments on other people's bodies a lot and shows me what an "appropriate" body should look like. i just want to make him proud. i don't want to be fat because he won't love me or care about me then. like my dad said, he is the only one who would truly love me.

dad keeps telling me he's the only one who loves me. what about my mom. what did i ever do to her? i keep thinking, where is mom? why isn't she here? she has to know about everything. i start blaming her. i don't want anything to do with her. i had no one. my dad told me my mom didn't care about me. everything is always about him. dad told me mom was mean and he was protecting me from her. i asked about my brudder and sister and he just told me "don't worry about them." the lies spilled out of his mouth like the church songs on sunday mornings.

i am confused.

everyone loved my mom. how is she mean?

"can i go to _____'s house?"
"no. we have a playdate." (playdate was code for i had to see the other people who were paying my dad to do whatever they wanted with me).
"i don't want to have a playdate today." *starts crying.*

"you ungrateful piece of trash. you are always making my life harder. you don't ever want to make me happy after everything i do for you. i'm disappointed in you."
"i'm sorry."
"you're in trouble tonight." whenever he said i was in trouble i knew it was going to be a bad.
"i'm sorry."
"i love you. you know i'm only trying to look out for you right?"

i hated when dad was disappointed in me. i just want to make him proud. i just want to make mom proud. i just want people to like me because then at least someone would. i don't even like myself. i feel dirty. i feel disgusting. maybe dad is right about me. i probably am really worth nothing.

dad branded me. "marking my property" he said. dad was right. i was his property. i will forever have a "j" on my body. i don't even know who i am. somedays i was allowed to do what i wanted to do. most days i had "playdates" or did what my dad wanted. i never knew which day it was going to be. i could wake up and have a good day where nothing abusive happened and other days i would be numbed out all day internally singing my abc's. i always walked on eggshells. i always found myself apologizing for things i didn't do. when a gun was being held up to me, i would wish it would go off. being drugged so i wouldn't fight back. things are blurry. i don't remember some things but maybe that's a good thing?

"you know you're getting a little chunky and people don't want to pay as much."
"i'm sorry."
dad tells me i'm built like a man and restricts some of my food.

no wonder no one likes me. i'm everyone's doormat and just a lame piece of property. i belong to other people. my body isn't mine. who am i?
dad took me to a hotel to meet one of the guys who paid for me. i grabbed the teddy bear i brought tightly. i don't know what's going to happen. i feel funny inside. i don't know if it was the alcohol he gave me before hand or the smell of mari-juana in the room. my dad dropped me off,

"make me proud."

dad left. the man took my hand and walked me to the bed. He started taking his clothes off. tears silently went down my face. I don't want to do this anymore. "why are you crying? you're gonna ruin the moment." the man threw me on the bed and started raping me. i kept thinking to myself "make it stop. please..."

abcdefghijklmnopqrstuvwxyz now i know my abc's next time won't you sing with me...

the room started going dizzy. my eyes are blurry. i don't know what is happening to me. my chest is getting tighter and tighter. i can't speak. i can't scream. i can't breathe. he's heavy. i can't move him off me. i start hitting him. i can't breathe. the man is now mad and frustrated with me. i'm sorry. he hits me again. i start going in and out of consciousness.
everything goes black.
my body is lifeless. he doesn't notice.
i don't make a sound.
i don't fight back.

he moved my limp body and knew something was wrong. he called my dad and started apologizing. i feel like i'm a fly in the corner of a room watching everything. my body is lifeless on the bed. my dad comes in and moves me to the ground. he looks pale. the guy kept apologizing. my dad started cpr. what's happening? there's a light. i don't want to wake up. i feel at peace. don't bring me back. dad continues to do cpr and i let out a huge gasp. i kept gasping for air like i forgot how to breathe. my dad and this man are staring at me. oh my God. i'm going to get in trouble. my body tenses up in fear. someone is going to hit me. someone is going to do something. i shouldn't have tried fighting back. all of a sudden, my dad hugged me. what was happening? am i not going to get in trouble? i'm so confused. i saw the guy give my dad double of what he was going to give him...$2000. that was the most i was ever worth until it happened again.

"that was thrilling wasn't it?"

the words that came from my dad's mouth. he cleaned me up, i put on a smile, he grabbed my hand and we walked out of the hotel. i lost my teddy bear that day...

my dad continues to give me to other people for profit and continues to abuse me himself until around age thirteen. i don't want to be alive anymore.

please make it stop.

STOP.

Breathe in. Breathe out.
Take some time for yourself.
Here is my favorite grounding technique:

- What are five things you can feel? What are the texture's like? Soft? Hard? What does it feel like? Is it cold? Neutral? Hot? Describe what you feel.

_____

_____

_____

_____

_____

- What are four things you can see? What do they look like? Is it colorful? Does it look like it has some texture? Describe what you see.

_____

_____

_____

_____

_____

- What are three things you can hear? What does it sound like? Is it loud? Quiet? Describe what you hear.

_____

_____

_____

- What are two things you can smell? What does it smell like? Describe what you smell.

_____

_____

- What is one thing you can taste? Describe what you taste.

_____

_____

CHAPTER THREE:

hurricane.

my family lived in a two-bedroom mobile home in southwest florida. we were the last house on the left down an old dirt road. the house had a screened in patio where my siblings and i would play a lot. my dad used one of the bedrooms as his computer rooms. he had filing cabinets everywhere and his desk was hidden in the back of the room. his bathroom was sponge bob themed. i know, random. the living room had a couch separating the dining room and a big chair on the right side of the wall. there was a tv up against the wall where we would watch family guy. the second bathroom was themed in black bears. the bedroom where we all slept was quite crowded. on one side of the room there was a wooden bunkbed. i slept on the top bunk and my little sister slept on the bottom. on the other side of the room, there was a white metal bunkbed. my brudder slept on top while my mom and dad slept on the futon underneath. our dog slept wherever she could find a space. there was hardly any space to move around. because we all slept in the one bedroom, it wasn't abnormal to see everyone naked. we were used to seeing each other undress and walk around naked.

in august of 2004, a hurricane made a last-minute turn and it destroyed the town i grew up in. during the middle of the night my dad woke us kids up and told us we had to go to my grandparents (paternal) house. i was half asleep and did not want to leave the house. i was pissed. we get to my paternal grandparents' house and wait out the storm moving from one end of the house to the other. we sat in the bathtub with a mattress over our head to protect us from the falling ceiling. we lost power. in fact, the whole town lost power. there were trampolines flying across the yards. it was unbelievable. after the hurricane was over, my mom and dad went to check on our house.

"it's gone." were the words that came from my mom's mouth.

my mom and dad couldn't even drive through our neighborhood. they had to walk and climb over trees and debris. when us kids were allowed to come out to see the house a couple days later, i couldn't believe what i saw.

there were stairs leading up to absolutely nothing. our house was in piles of debris in our neighbors' yard and my neighbors' house in our yard. the house behind us was cut in half. apparently, a tornado came out of the hurricane while it was happening. i looked and saw my wooden bed completely flipped upside down dug into the ground.

i felt sad.

not because my bed was gone or because my house was gone. but because i could have been dug into the ground too. dead. the abuse would have stopped. i would have finally been free.

i remember one of my stuffed animals, a white cat i named louise, was in mud in the ground. i went to pick her up and try to sneak her into the car. my parents found her each time. my stuffed animals were gone. my trophies that i earned were ruined. the only stuffed animal i had left was an emerald green bear i named birthstone.

the only clothes my family had were the ones my mom left in the washer and dryer before we left. my family was home-less among many others in my small town. ironically, my water shoes stayed in the exact location during the entire hurricane. i don't know how.

my paternal grandparents allowed us to live with them until we could find a place to live. during the time we lived with my grandparents, my grandpa began molesting me and raping me. at this point, i was not even phased. i don't know if my dad knew what my grandpa was doing. sometimes my grandma would give me lingerie and tell me to go in front of my grandpa. the grandkids would walk around their house naked and exposed because it was normal. one day my mom walked in on my grandpa molesting me and my mom asked my dad about it and my dad told her it was nothing and to not be concerned. my dad used his manipulative words once again to protect himself.

eventually my parents found a dutchman travel trailer for us to live in. we parked it in front of my grandparents' house in their driveway until we were able to get a new house. the trailer was pretty neat. unfortunately, the abuse continued in the trailer. i became to resent that trailer. when it was parked in front of our new home sometimes i would go to the trailer to escape but then it became a place for my dad to take me to rape me.

we got a new mobile home where our old house used to be. this house was so big compared to our previous one. we now lived in a four-bedroom, two bath mobile home. it had two living rooms, a dining room, kitchen, and laundry room. my siblings and i each had our own rooms with walk in closets. we were so used to living in a small space that my siblings and i each sat in our closets for a while. we always played in our closets—they were kind of our safe place. whenever a thunderstorm would come and shake the house, we were terrified and ran to our parents' bedroom or wherever they were at the time. the hurricane was traumatizing.

the new house was fun at first. it was like we were staying at a hotel. we played a lot and had a big dirt hill out back. my brudder and i would take our bikes and ride down the dirt hill. we would bring the hose out and make mud. it was so fun. my brudder, sister, and i played pretend a lot. it was my escape. i would pretend i was in a different world. i loved writing stories for that reason. i usually wrote about a girl who would run away and find an amazing life. there were always a lot of animals and my brudder was there. my brudder is my best friend.

my brudder and i could communicate without even talking. we had a special bond…a trauma bond. sometimes my brudder and i would sleep in my mom and dad's room and my mom would be sleeping and my dad would be at his computer watching child pornography. my brudder and i both knew it. were bad things happening to him too? i have to protect him. i have to protect my sister. i'm the oldest. it's my job.

when we moved into the new house, i thought the abuse with my grandpa would stop. i thought we wouldn't have to go over to my grandparents' house as often. i was wrong. again. the abuse with my grandpa continued. i would beg my dad to not go to my grandparents' house. his response wasn't any better. when he would go to drop off my siblings at my grandparents' house, dad would say, "when i get back you better be naked." when i wasn't naked when he got back, i got hit. at least with my dad i semi knew what to expect. it was more comfortable because it has been happening longer.

does dad know what is going on with grandpa? i don't want my dad to get mad and my grandpa to get in trouble. i'm not going to say anything. i can't.

one night my family and i were all watching movies in one of the living rooms and we brought all the mattresses out. we had a huge family sleepover. it was fun until dad started having sex with me when everyone fell asleep. i'm scared mom is going to wake up. she's going to be mad at me. i have to be quiet.

abcdefghijklmnopqrstuvwxyz now i know my abc's next time won't you sing with me.

i disassociated.

i can't feel anything.

this doesn't feel right.

i feel dirty.

i feel disgusting.

i hate myself. i hate myself so much.

why does this keep happening? i don't know what i keep doing to make this keep happening. why couldn't i have died in the hurricane? i don't want to be here...

i'm starting to feel again. i start fighting. dad hits me. i lay limp. i can't stop crying. i have to be quiet. i lay there silently crying. i want to go home.

…the worst part is. i am home.

i want my mom. how does she not know? I'm so confused. i'm so angry. i hate feeling angry. when i'm angry i get in trouble.

angry equals bad.

i am bad.

Self-discovery prompt:

Use the next two pages to make a collage of where you are in your life right now and where you want to be. What goals do you have? How will you grow?

CHAPTER FOUR:

silence.

when i was in third grade, i was playing on the playground. i wanted to stay with the teachers. i felt more comfortable around adults. i felt like i didn't really get along with kids my age. i felt like i didn't understand kids my age. when the teacher went to check on one of the other kids, i was walking behind her. i was talking to her like she could hear me (she couldn't). i said, "someone told me that if i held my breath, i could make my face turned purple. want to see?" i liked purple. i held my breath. my heart started beating. i could feel my heart beating in my head. i've felt this feeling before in the hotel room. everything went black. i passed out. the teacher turned around and i was laying on the mulch. i got up, the teacher gave me carrots, and i sat under the awning until it was time to go back inside. they called for my dad to come pick me up. dad picked me up and i got in trouble.

"how could you be so stupid? you know not to hold your breath that long. who even does that?"

"i'm sorry. i'm sorry."

dad laughed at me. dad was also yelling at me. i'm confused. is he mad or just playing around? sometimes it was hard to tell what dad was really feeling. usually i'm good at reading people so i know how to act. he was hard to read.

when i was home from school, dad set up more "playdates." the older i got, the trickier things would get. dad stopped calling them "playdates" and started calling them "appointments." of course it would sound natural when dad would tell mom or other people "i have to take meg to an appt." i just stayed quiet. there was nothing i could do to get out of it. nothing i could say. if i fought, i would just get hurt. there was no point. the appointments became longer the older i got. i feel like i missed a huge part of my life because i was numb and disassociated for most of it. numbing myself is an instinct. i don't know when that instinct started.

dad always told me that if i were to tell anyone about what he was doing with me, he would kill me. the more the abuse kept happening, the more i thought, "him killing me wouldn't be a bad thing." i was upset. upset that i haven't died before. there were plenty of times where i thought "this is it. this is going to be the time i won't make it." each time i came through. why? why can't i just die? why do i have to keep living like this? it's not fair.

my grandparents homeschooled my brother, sister, and i while i was in fourth and fifth grade because both of my parents worked. my mom was a preschool teacher and my dad worked at the landfill. it always felt like my grandparents hated me. when my grandma would go to the dollar tree and get the grandkids gifts, she would tell me, "i must have forgotten you." how could she forget about me? she would have me put lingerie on and go in front of my grandpa. i just want them to like me. i want them to notice me. what do i have to do for them to love me?

my dad reminded me when he would drop us off, "remember, if anyone finds out about our secret, i will kill you. i will kill your siblings and your mother." those words would play over and over again. they were great reminders until i wanted to die then i didn't care... i couldn't do that though. i couldn't let anything happen to my brudder, sister, and mom. i had to protect them. it was my job.

while i was being homeschooled, i would always finish my work within two or three hours. it was hard to keep me entertained. my grandparents got annoyed. when i started learning about fractions in math, i did not understand. i asked my grandparents for help and they refused to help me. i felt defeated. i felt dumb. why can't i understand this? as i continued with math, i started skipping sections and writing "idk" all over the page because i didn't know how to solve the problems. i started getting done with school even earlier. my grandparents were annoyed and would tell me to go play in the woods or go outside. i went in the woods with the plastic utensils i drew faces on and played. my imagination was wild. it was my escape.

one day my grandpa decided to check my schoolwork and when he got to my math book, he saw all of the "idk" pages and asked me what it was for. i told him i didn't know how to do it and no one would help me. grandpa got annoyed with me and slapped me. we spent hours going over my math work and i still didn't understand. my grandpa gave up. he was over it.

"you need to learn how to pay attention when someone is trying to teach you."

i don't understand math. how am i supposed to pay attention when i don't understand and just keep getting yelled at? i was so mad and felt so dumb. i hate math. i never want to do it again.

one night i spent the night at my aunt's house. when my aunt went to drop me off at my dad's work, the landfill, i was begging her to let me stay at her house just one more night. my aunt told me i couldn't stay with her. when we got to my dad's work i got out of the car and went up to the office. it wasn't until years later when my aunt told me she didn't feel comfortable leaving me. i wonder why. did she have concerns of abuse? i wonder if she said something if the abuse would have stopped.

when i got to the office, my dad introduced me to his coworkers. his tone of voice changed. i knew what was coming. my eyes started tearing up. i just wanted to be back at my aunt's house. my dad gives me a stern look that meant 'stop crying.' he's right. i have to be professional. i have to do what i'm told so dad is proud of me. so dad can get paid. maybe if i'm good this time i can get another stuffed animal. maybe dad will let me get make up this time. i've been wanting to wear mascara like my cousin. dad let one of his coworkers take me for a while. when we got back dad noticed a scratch on me.

"what happened to her?"

"she tried getting away and i was afraid she was going to say something."

"no i didn't. i promise daddy. i promise i didn't."

"get in the car."

i knew i was in trouble. i knew dad was mad. i don't talk the whole way home. we did not stop for a teddy bear. we did not stop for mascara. my eyes are watering. i don't know why dad's coworker said i tried getting away. i know better. i wouldn't do that. i need to be good.

the scratch came from myself.

i did it.

i needed to feel something. i needed a release.

dad stopped at the little trail/park on the way home. dad raped me. it was my punishment. i was bad. i feel disgusting. i feel gross. we get back in the car to head home. i don't talk. i have nothing to say. i want to be left alone. i don't want to be near anyone.

"i love you." were the words that came from my dad's mouth. i'm confused. how? is this what love is? it's not how i see it in the movies. well, the movies aren't real anyway. maybe this is what love is. i don't want to be "loved" anymore.

the next few days i was silent. mom asked me what was wrong. "i just don't feel good." i knew how to lie. if i told her, she would get hurt. i couldn't let that happen.

i was so bored being homeschooled i begged my parents to go to a public school. my parents decided we would all go to public school. i started sixth grade at the local middle school. my cousin was in the same school just a different grade. each morning my parents would drop us off at my grandparents' house. my grandparents would take my brother and sister to school then take my cousin and i to school. my cousin and i would get ready together. i always looked up to her. she was one of the cool kids. i was the awkward girl who was quiet and didn't know how to socialize. i didn't know how to make friends or act around people my age. i preferred to try to be friends with adults. i would always talk to the teachers. i would never mention anything about my personal life though. that's too dangerous. i knew what would happen if i did.

i started getting bullied by the more popular group of girls because i was too quiet. i would shut down even more. i was used to not being liked. during gym class i was so competitive. i would always try to beat the guys. i had to be perfect. if i wasn't perfect bad things happened. my favorite gym days was when we ran. i loved running. running became an outlet for me.

as i got older and started developing breasts, my dad became even more harsh towards my body. he would call me fat every day. tell me i was eating too much. i started skipping lunches at school.

dad would be proud.

instead of him portioning my food, i was learning how to do it myself. i felt empowered. i am finally able to control something.

during the mornings before my grandma took my cousin and i to school, i would weigh myself on her scale. it became a habit. when the number went down, i felt happier. i felt accomplished. i was finally doing something right. one morning my grandma told me to put lingerie on and go in front of my grandpa. i didn't want to. i started crying and i locked myself in her bathroom and sat in the shower until it was time to go to school.

i started becoming more and more depressed. i didn't know how to do standardized testing or how to write with paragraphs because my grandparents never taught me when i was homeschooled. my dad noticed i was getting depressed. he asked me why.

"because girls are being mean to me at school."
"we need to go tell someone."
"no. dad. please. i can handle it."
"no one messes with my baby girl."

after school was let out one day, dad brings me back in. we go to the main office and he asks to speak to someone because his daughter is getting bullied. the sixth-grade guidance counselor comes out and brings me back to her office. the guidance counselor was pretty. she felt safe. i was really good at feeling people out. we get to her office and the lights are dim. it is cozy. i start crying. my anxiety is through the roof. does she know about my dad?

"what's going on, sweetie?"
"my dad wants me to tell you about people bullying me"
as i talk with the guidance counselor about the details of getting bullied, she looks at me and asks, "is there anything else you want to talk about today?"
my brain is screaming. i start crying. tell her meghan! tell her what dad is doing. yes, my dad is raping me and selling me to people.
words would not come out. only thoughts. i can't talk. my brain is screaming. i want to talk so bad but nothing is coming out. i'm frozen. my anxiety gets the best of me. i can't betray my dad. i can't be that daughter. i have to be good. i can't do this,

"no, i'm okay. thank you though."

the guidance counselor looks at me concerned. "okay. let's bring you out to your dad." the guidance counselor takes me back to my dad and my dad sees that i have been crying. he gives me a look. dad is mad. what did i do? i didn't tell. i didn't betray him. we get to the car.

"why are you crying?"

"i didn't say anything, i promise. i didn't tell her anything about the secret."

dad looked relieved.

i could have been free that day. that could have been the end. the abuse could have stopped. there wouldn't have to be anymore secrets. but i was too scared. i couldn't betray my dad.

i couldn't do it.

Journal prompt:

Write about a time/times in your life when you wanted to say something but were afraid. What did you feel? Were you negative towards yourself? Were you ashamed? Write what you were going to say.

_____

_____

_____

_____

_____

_____

_____

_____

_____

_____

_____

_____

CHAPTER FIVE:
merely surviving. I'm done.

my parents decided that we were going to be homeschooled again because i was getting bullied. my dad lost his job and stayed at home to homeschool us while my mom worked full-time to provide for the family. during this time, the abuse started happening everyday while my mom was at work. most days after school, my dad would bring my brother and sister to my grandparents and i would have to go to my "appointments." i would beg my dad to not let me go to my grandparents' house. when my cousins were at grandma and grandpa's house i would rather go because i could play with them.

one day when my brother and sister were taking a bath, my dad was having sex with me. my grandma (paternal) walked into our house without knocking and came into my parents' bedroom. my dad quickly got up and ran to the closet. i was laying in the bed, naked, extremely embarrassed. my grandma was having a normal conversation with me like she didn't see anything. i was under the covers trying to put my clothes on so she wouldn't notice anything. i didn't want my dad to get in trouble. i was terrified.

what if she saw something?

what if she found out about dad's secret?

in seventh grade where i am from, usually in school we are taught about sex education. when i was in seventh grade, i was homeschooled, my dad taught me about space and the planets. i had no idea about anything sex education related. only what my dad is doing to me. i am so naive in a way. how am i supposed to know what my dad is doing isn't right? i grew up with sexual and physical abuse happening to me my whole life. i started cutting myself more in seventh grade to relieve feelings and to feel something because i was so numb. i cut myself sporadically all over my body so my dad didn't know what i was doing. my dad told me about a time when he would cut himself. he told me it started when he found his brother dead and showed me his scars. i asked him, "what would you do if i ever started cutting myself?" dad told me, "i would beat you so hard. i wouldn't love you anymore." i couldn't let dad find out. i don't care about the beatings because he already did that. if dad didn't love me, no one else would. i can't do something to make him not love me anymore.

i had a secret of my own now.

my brudder and i were playing a game with my dad one day. we were taking turns building a fort in the house. when it was my turn to build the fort, my dad would go to his computer and wait for it to be my brudder's turn. when it was my brudder's turn to build the fort, my dad would take me into my bedroom and lock the door. my dad took my clothes off and began touching me. every time he touched me i felt dirty.

i felt uncomfortable, no matter how many times he's touched me before. my dad began raping me. i lay there silent. i don't make a sound because i need to protect my brudder.

abcdefghijklmnopqrstuvwxyz now i know my abc's next time won't you sing with me. i disassociate. i can't feel a thing. dad is done. my turn to build the fort now.

there was one time i stopped the abuse. my dad was raping me in his room and i was yelling "i hate you" over and over again. he stopped and walked away. i ran to my bedroom. i sat by the window crying, wishing i could escape. my dad comes in my room. am i going to get in trouble? i'm not supposed to talk back, let alone yell at him and tell him i hate him. my dad started talking—"i'm sorry." what? what does he mean i'm sorry? i'm the one that misbehaved and yelled at him. i should be apologizing to him.

as i got older, my dad let me do more things by myself. he trusted me. that felt good. i did something right. i am good. my dad let me join a girls club called gems. it stood for girls everywhere meeting the savior. this club was every thursday night at the church where my mom worked. on wednesday nights i would help with the dinners the church cooked. there was an adult there that i trusted and felt like i related to. i was in my room one night texting her after gems and then called her. we were talking and i was crying and it slipped out what my dad had been doing to me. she told me i needed to tell someone or else she will. i felt betrayed. she told me that whatever i told her would stay between us.

dad always told me if i ever told anyone he would kill me along with everyone i loved. a part of me felt relieved. i don't care if he killed me. it would be better than living the life i am "living." but i can't let everyone i love die.

i start panicking.

i screwed up. what did i do? oh my gosh, my mom is going to die and my brudder and sister. i killed them. i'm such a screw up. i can't save my dad now.

thursday, march 4, 2010—the day my life changed forever... my mom eventually came in to check on me because it was cold in the house and i had been gone for a while. when mom walked into the room, she saw me crying and asked me what was wrong. i told her "nothing" and tried to get away with that answer. she then began asking me questions, "did you delete your text messages?" (i wasn't allowed to delete my text messages at the time), "did you do something you shouldn't have?" i kept shaking my head no. finally, mom asked, "did someone hurt you?" i froze. oh my gosh. what am i supposed to say now? mom, why do you have to keep asking questions you're going to get me in trouble! i barely shook my head yes. she then started asking who is was and finally asked if it was my dad. i broke down crying and told her what dad has been doing to me (only the bare minimum though). i was terrified.

next thing i know, dad is coming in my room holding a knife. i went into panic mode and started freaking out. this was it. dad said he would kill me if i ever told about what he has been doing to me and i just told my mom. i ran underneath my bed and hid with tears streaming down my face in a complete panic. little did i know that dad was doing the dishes and went back and put the knife down. dad came back and mom asked him if he had been raping me. my dad obviously said no and appeared to be confused. my mom and dad went into my brudder's room and talked for a little. about forty-five minutes to an hour later, mom came back in my room saying she did not know who to believe anymore. dad asked if he could speak with me privately, but my mom told him that she was going to be right there with me.

i still didn't feel safe. mom has been with me my whole life. how is she supposed to protect me against my dad? somehow i knew that if I didn't stand up for myself, then the abuse would get a lot worse. i had to protect myself. what if mom didn't believe me and dad didn't kill us. i don't know how things could get worse but they probably would. dad is full of surprises.

Out of nowhere, a sense of fire came rushing through my veins and I got an overwhelming sense of strength and courage. I felt strong for the first time in my life. I felt a sense of control. Where is this coming from? My mom, dad, and I were all sitting on my bed talking trying to figure out who was telling the truth. I looked my dad straight in the eyes and told him, "you know what you did. Have the balls like a real man and admit to it." My dad was shocked. Who is she? My dad broke down crying and continuously repeated, "I'm so sorry. I'm so sorry." Throughout the years I realized he was crying because he got caught, not because he was actually sorry. However, in the moment, it felt nice to be apologized to. My brudder and sister were outside of the door trying to hear what was going on.

after the three of us got done talking for the night, we all went to bed. mom took my sister and i into her room to sleep while brudder slept on the pullout couch with my dad. the next morning, friday, march 5, 2010, my dad put all of the sheets from the house into the wash. the five of us went to my mom's work where my dad and mom talked to the pastor trying to figure out what to do. "if a family member molested another family member, what would be the next steps to take?" meanwhile, my brudder, sister, and i were playing on the playground. i texted the adult i trusted to tell her that i told my mom so she didn't have to (it was years before I understood that the adult I trusted was required—by law—to tell someone about what was happening).

we were at my mom's work for a few hours and then my mom's boss guessed it was me that they had been talking about. my mom's boss offered to call the police so my mom wouldn't have to and next thing i know, we were on our way back home. the ride home was very awkward. what have i done?! i texted my mom asking if dad was going to jail and she replied with, "yes." a huge sense of relief was lifted from my shoulders, however, a giant wave of guilt also flooded over me. how could I betray my dad like that? i'm a horrible person. i can't be trusted. dad is going to suffer in jail now because of me and that isn't fair for him. so many untrue thoughts flooded my brain but they sure as hell felt true to me. i then started thinking about my mom. what is she feeling? is she mad at me? how could i take my dad away from her and my siblings?

when we get home, we took a family walk around our neighborhood. my mom and dad talked while my brudder, sister, and i played and walked. when we finished the walk and made it back home, my dad kept wanting to go back outside. mom was stopping him asking him what was behind his back. things escalated and brudder got scared and hid all the knives in my parent's bathroom. dad kept asking to go outside— apparently, he had a gun behind his back and was going to shoot himself. mom calmed him down enough to where she got the gun and dad went and sat on the couch with his head in his hands between his knees, crying. my sister and brudder and i stood there watching. i didn't know what to do. i did this. i'm ruining all of our lives.

my dad walked up to my brudder and told him that he has to be the man of the house now and had to protect us. dad walked up to my sister and told her that he is going to be gone for a while and my sister was confused. she's only nine so how can she understand? i couldn't even really comprehend what all was happening. finally, dad walked up to me and asked if he could have a hug. i didn't want to give him a hug but i felt awful for what i was doing to him. i was frozen. i owed it to him. i could not move. i could not speak. what is wrong with me? dad didn't wait for me to answer, he gave me a hug anyway. once again violated my space one last time. dad walked out the door and turned himself in that day. march 5, 2010.

Years later, I found out that my dad wanted to turn himself in so that he could "protect us kids and not hurt us by having us see him getting taken away in the police car."

insert sarcasm dad of the year award goes to…mine!

when dad left, we all stood there and did not know what to do. that day was the last day i ever saw him. my dad's parents came over to be with us during this hard time; however, i still did not tell about my paternal grandpa's abuse at this time. i was scared and couldn't even think about letting anyone know about my grandpa and grandma. i do have to say, the grandparents put on a great act of trying to 'protect' us when my dad was taken away. a little bit after my grandparents came over, the detectives showed up.

the detectives walked me through each room in the house and asked if my dad raped me there. i answered "yes." when we got to my parent's bedroom, one of the detectives asked me where the sheets to the bed went. i responded obliviously with, "oh he washed them this morning" and anxiously laughed. the detective responded with, "of course he did." i was really confused as to why she said that. did i get dad in even more trouble? ugh, why can't i just keep my mouth shut?

it wasn't until later when i realized that dad washed the sheets to cover up evidence…

i wake up the next morning at my dad's parents' house with a sense of heaviness. i feel awful. I feel like a horrible daughter. I don't know how to go on without my dad. how am i supposed to live? how am i supposed to function? it feels like there is a big hole in my heart. a knot in my stomach. how is my dad doing? is he ok? is dad mad at me? what is he feeling? i had so many questions. so many questions i will never get the answers to. i don't know what's going to happen to me. are the guys my dad sold me to going to find me?

i feel lost. i don't like this. i made a mistake.

The day of and the day after I told about my abuse, we were supposed to do a workday and get free Disney passes. We did not make it and never went to Disney. Instead, my family is trying to find our new normal.

There were many doctors' appointments, rape kits, talking to detectives, and reliving my childhood over and over again until my dad was finally charged. Dad was charged with four life sentences but took the plea bargain and is sentenced to twenty-five years. Dad could also get out early for good behavior and only has to serve eighty percent of his sentence. When talking to the detectives, I did not tell about my "appointments" and dad selling me. i did not know what all to say. i was numb. i was betraying my dad. i felt like i was getting in trouble. Maybe if I would have told the detectives, dad would have gotten his four life sentences he was originally charged with. My mind still wonders how someone could admit to being guilty and then get a shorter sentence. The justice system isn't just. I still get confused. I still get bitter. I was very angry with my mom because she started dating the detective on my dad's case when it was going on. She could have gotten it thrown out. What was she thinking? I was very upset and started acting out.

Days passed. Weeks passed. Fun fact, I never finished seventh grade.

When my dad's case closed and he went to prison, my maternal grandma came down to Florida to help mom out. It was nice having her here but I do not really remember it. I was numb—just going through the motions of life. I lost my dad. He was the biggest part of my life. Why did I have to ruin everything? I remember sitting at the table with my grandma and out of nowhere she told me she was so proud of me.

me...

how could she be proud of me after i destroyed my family? my grandma told me a little about her past and the words, "i wish i could have been as strong as you and told about what happened to me, i still haven't told anyone" came out of her mouth. i didn't understand. what was so great about me telling? a part of me felt sad. sad that my grandma had to live her whole life with the secret of what happened to her. she did not go into details but made sure i knew she was so proud of me.

I finally got to a point where I was so numb, I was ready to tell about my paternal grandpa. I called my mom one day when I was going to the bathroom and told her about what my grandpa did to me. Next thing I know, we were back to square one with the police. More detectives. More questioning. More being forced to be vulnerable. when i was in eighth grade, i had to go down to the police station to do a controlled phone call to my grandpa. when i got to the station, the detective that was on my case had me go into a room with her. there was a phone, a desk, and two chairs. it was a small room. she explained to me that she was going to be with me the whole time and if i ever got stuck, to look at her and she would help me. the goal was to get my grandpa to confess.

she dialed the number and my grandpa picked up, "hello."

"hi grandpa, this is meghan."

"oh hi, how are you?"

i froze. i can't do this. i looked to the detective and she wrote on paper, "tell him you're sick from school." i feel bad lying. i can't do this. but i have to do it. i've already come this far.

"i'm ok. i'm home sick from school."

"oh, that's a bummer."

"yea." i took a long pause. "so i was thinking about everything that happened to me with dad and then i started thinking more and was wondering why you raped me too?"

"what?! i never did that!"

i started panicking. what do i do? i looked over to the detective for some help. she told me to breathe and that i'm safe with her.

"grandpa, you know what you did." my voice was shaking. next thing i know, the detective and i hear my grandma in the background. why was she home? she was supposed to be at bible study. we heard her telling my grandpa what to say in the background. we went back and forth for a little bit. finally, i got the courage again to stand up to my grandpa. the same fire was burning inside me as it was when i was standing up to my dad.

"grandpa, dad was a man and confessed to it. have the balls and be like him. you know what you did."

"i never hurt you. the only thing i remember was when i was sleeping, you would take my hand and touch yourself with it. touch your private parts"

"oh really?"

"yes. that's what happened."

i got pissed and started going off on him...

"how old was I grandpa? about six? maybe seven?"

"yea. about six or seven."

"grandpa, why would a six or seven-year-old take your hand and touch themselves with it?"

"i don't know but that's what happened. that's what you did."

i started getting angry and stood up. the detective told me to calm down and that we got him and there was enough information to arrest him. she told me I could be done talking with him and to hang up and calm down.

"grandpa, I gotta go."

*hangs up the phone."

the detective told me i did a good job. when they went to arrest my grandpa, all of the detectives at the station wanted to go and get him because they were all pissed and invested in my case. all of sudden, i remember feeling awful. there I go again, putting another family member in jail. destroying the family even more.

months went by and we got a call to go into the station. they sat mom and i down and told us that there isn't enough information on my grandpa's case and that if no one else speaks up, they're going to have to drop the case. my mom emailed many of my grandparent's foster kids and explained to them what was going on. she asked if anyone had information or abusive experiences with my grandpa or grandma then to please speak up. no one did. my case was dropped.

i went numb. i felt inadequate. embarrassed. pissed. scared. like none of my experiences were valid or true. i began cutting myself and starving myself even more to help myself stay numb and focused on something else because it was better than feeling what I was feeling. years went by. in about 2017 or 2018, someone emailed my mom back and told her that she was also molested. i was angry. why couldn't she have talked sooner? I know you are all probably thinking that I'm inconsiderate for thinking that but it's what was going on through my head in the moment. I understand that it's really not easy to tell and even after telling about my dad, I still waited years to tell about my grandpa.

My mom separated my brudder, sister, and I from my dad's side of the family for protection. She did not trust any of them. i felt awful. i destroyed my family. The first holiday was the hardest. Holidays used to be at my grandparents' house and the entire family would come together. I got to see aunts and uncles I never got the chance to see. Holidays now consisted of my mom, brudder, sister, and I. It was odd. Uncomfortable. I was not getting abused on holidays anymore. I was not getting abused on my dad's birthday. I was not getting abused ever.

What is this life?

JOURNAL PROMPT:

Write 10 affirmations about yourself.
Think on the inside, dig deep.

1. _____

_____

2. _____

_____

3. _____

_____

4. _____

_____

5. _____

_____

6. _____

_____

7. _____

_____

8. _____

_____

9.

_____

_____

10.

_____

_____

CHAPTER SIX:

my new world.

i'm lost.

what do i do when i don't have anyone constantly controlling me?

watching my every move?

how am i supposed to act?

what am i supposed to feel?

i don't know how to live.

Days turned into weeks and weeks turned into months. I started therapy and writing letters to my dad that never got sent. It was supposed to be a coping tool but I really did want to talk to him. My dad sent me letters telling me everything was my fault. i believed them. A no contact order indefinitely was placed and one of my homework assignments for therapy was to burn the letters from my dad. I burnt them all but still felt empty inside. am i always going to feel this way? i thought i was supposed to feel empowered. someone please tell me how to feel.

how did my life become the way it is? one day we were a family and the next day, my entire world changed. At first my trauma response was to the change because being abused and sold was normal for me. In a way, I missed it. I missed the consistency and routine. I missed my dad.

I took everything out on myself—not only my emotions but everyone else's emotions too. I felt responsible. i mean, it was my fault that he was in jail in the first place. I cut myself a lot. I burned myself a lot. I restricted my food a lot. it was all my fault. my mom is now a single mom because of me. my siblings don't have a dad because of me. i hate myself. i wanted my dad back. I carved a "j" into my body because I missed my dad so much that I wanted a part of him with me. it was my way of letting myself know i am still his. I know that sounds crazy, but it made sense at the time.

I was in the guidance counselors at school every day. Crying. Trying to find a sense of self. I got attached. I felt safe. What was this? I became really good friends with her daughter and we hung out all the time. I was allowed to go to friends' houses. I was allowed to have fun. i felt bad for having fun. I remember being at my friend's house and having really bad anxiety and crying because I had "stretch marks." I showed her my stretch marks and she told me, "those are not stretch marks, those are veins. these are stretch marks." She showed me what stretch marks looked like. i didn't believe her. i was fat. i ate too much. my dad would be ashamed of me.

The guidance counselor and I still talk to this day.

It was hard trying to go to school and pretend like I'm not going through anything. i don't want people to ask questions. i don't want people to feel bad for me. i just want to be normal. at least when my dad was here, what he was doing was normal for me. when other kids talked about their dad and families it brought up a lot of guilt and anger. if i didn't say anything, my family would still be together. Instead of being numb all the time, I started being an emotional person. I hated it. When I try to bottle all my emotions up, they would burst out eventually. This never happened growing up. What is going on?

I became very depressed and decided one night I was going to end my life. I was cutting myself to cope and when my therapist was talking to me, I was done. I wanted to die. My therapist decided to baker act (commit) me and next thing I know I am in the back of a police car trying to suffocate myself as I am being taken to a psychiatric hospital. I got there and am terrified. What is this place? I refused to eat. I refused to talk. I met with a psychiatrist and was put on medications for the first time. The facility had a point system for good behavior and my need to put my worth in numbers only grew. I learned different unhealthy coping skills in the hospital. During meal one night, one of the other girls attacked me. my brain believed "i am bad." "food is bad." I know it doesn't make any sense, but it did to me.

when my therapist called me in the hospital, i felt cared for. i am mad at my therapist for sending me to the hospital but it was the first time i felt someone care about me. In reality, I sent myself there.

after i got out of the hospital and went back to therapy, i asked if we could walk during our session. i can't sit still. i have to move. she taught me what my dad is. a predator. i don't believe her though. how could my dad be a bad person? he told me he was the only one who cared about me and the only one who ever would. i started to not trust my therapist. when my therapist told me she had to move and couldn't work with me anymore, i lost all trust again. therapist after therapist i would continue being let down. i don't want to talk anymore. i don't need to work through anything. i'm fine.

I started opening up more to people who proved to me they were safe. I was not as quiet as I was growing up. At first I was scared. Someone told me once, "you're so quiet." I responded with, "you should have seen me a few years ago." I felt like i've grown so much. am i being too quiet? have i grown enough? am i doing something wrong? how am i supposed to talk? i don't have any direction anymore. i don't know what to do. my brain overthinks everything.

The summer before high school I continued to act out with self-harm and restricting my food. I didn't want to be here without my dad. I snuck out one night to drink with a friend and go to a party. I got drunk. I couldn't say no. I was gang raped by three guys that night. things finally felt normal. i was numb again. i continued mutilating myself to feel. my dad was no longer abusing me but i took on that role and continued to abuse myself. i continued the abuse through self-mutilation and starvation. i carved the word "fat" into my body, twice. i was mad at myself for being what i considered "overweight."

one night i became so overwhelmed with self-hate that i took a bottle of pills to try to end my life for the second time. i was starting to feel dizzy and extremely lightheaded. my heart was racing in my chest. something inside of me told me to get my mom. i told her what i did. she called a friend whose husband was a doctor and they met us at the hospital. i don't remember what happened but i woke up in an ambulance on the way to a psychiatric hospital. i get there and would not talk. my mom drove an hour to see me but i wouldn't talk to her. i was angry. angry at the world. angry at my mom. angry at myself. i refused to eat. i started throwing up blood at the facility. the nurses checked me out. i went to lay down. i tried to stay in my room as much as possible. i didn't want to be around anyone. the staff would try to force me to eat, i refused. i needed control. i started hiding my food. this habit only became worse. when i got out of the hospital. i felt embarrassed. "you're only doing this for attention" people would tell me.

no.

i wanted to die. i felt embarrassed. i felt like i let people down. i let my dad down. i let myself down. my need to be perfect only grew.

In high school, I attached myself to my teachers. They were safe. They were older. I felt more comfortable with older people than I did with people my age. i feel like people my age don't understand me. i feel awkward and like i don't belong. when i talk to my teachers, a part of me feels like i belong. i feel seen.

I got really close with my math teacher. I began going to her classroom in the morning's before school. It was my safe haven. I became her teacher's aide and assisted with grading papers to one of her classes I was not in. One year I had her during the period my lunch was in. I began staying in her classroom during lunch. i hated lunch. the cafeteria was too crowded. it was too loud. it made my anxiety around food even worse. My teacher asked if I was eating. I told her "sometimes." Sometimes I would eat with her but a lot of times she went to the teachers' lounge for lunch. My math teacher became pregnant and had her daughter eight weeks early. We still talk to this day. I still go to her for life advice.

Throughout the years I also started to become really involved in my youth group. I became one of the student leaders for middle schoolers. I helped lead a middle school girls group. Being a leader helped deepen my relationship with God. I would not have gotten this far in my journey if I didn't lean on God. Growing up, I became super mad at Him. if God controlled everything, why did he let my dad do the things he did? It wasn't until I learned about free will. That God was actually sad when I was sad. God was with me when my dad was raping and selling me. I learned that God didn't want those bad things to happen. I started looking to God as my father instead of my earthly dad. It was still hard though because I longed for a physical dad. I realized that the fire in my veins when I was speaking out against my dad and grandpa was God giving me the strength. There is nothing else that can explain it. I wouldn't be alive today if it wasn't for God—He has a bigger plan for my life.

After my dad was taken away, I would continuously go from father figure to father figure. When they didn't live up to my expectations of what a dad would be like, I got hurt. i saw what a dad was supposed to be like in movies. why wasn't mine like that? it's not fair. It wasn't until I found peace in the fact that I don't need an earthly father to live a great life. I took that peace and my main motivation became using my story of abuse to help others. Yes, I still get sad on Father's day and other holidays, but I am finally starting to apply healthy coping skills when I am triggered.

At this point in my journey, my brain isn't ready to process the trauma yet. It is trying to survive.

Journal prompt:

Use this page to draw something representing what you want to be remembered for.

CHAPTER SEVEN:

freedom through dance.

When I was in eighth grade, I fell in love with the idea of being a dancer. I did all of my projects on dance. My computer teacher asked me if I was involved in a studio and I told her, "I was when I was little but I am not now. But I wish I was." After school, one of the other computer teachers came to me and told me about a local dance studio her daughter, Michelle, teaches. She gave me a business card and told me to check it out. When I got home, I told my mom about it and begged her to try it. She agreed. I went to my first lyrical class a few weeks later.

I walked into the studio with my anxiety through the roof. what was i doing here? i'm too fat to be a dancer. why am i even trying this? I went into class and a woman named Andrea was teaching. She welcomed me and encouraged me through the class. I had no idea what I was doing but I tried anyway. I kept looking at the other girls trying not to compare myself and trying to just focus on the moves. The class already started their dance for their end of the year showtime. i felt awkward—like people were mad at me for joining so late. i had no idea what i was doing. i'm going to ruin the dance. After class,

Andrea came up to me and said, "you did a really good job for it being your first time." why isn't she criticizing me? why isn't she being mean to me? maybe i will like it here.

I got home and practiced and practiced the dance. I did the warmups we did in class at home to strengthen my muscles. I began to get to know the other girls in the class. They were nice to me. It was weird at first. I was never someone who had a lot of friends because I was so quiet. Showtime came around and I performed on stage in front of a bunch of people. My makeup was done, I was wearing a costume, and it was the most magical thing I've ever experienced. I danced when I was little (ironically at the same studio) but my dad took me out and I don't remember it at all.

I was always dancing in the house. I sat with my leg up by my head because it was comfortable. I practiced different moves in the house and may have broken a few lightbulbs while at it. If I was upset or triggered, I would put music on and dance. My favorite style is lyrical.

The next year I added a couple more classes to my schedule, jazz and ballet. I wanted to be on the competition team and in order to do that, I needed to take ballet and jazz as well. I was definitely out of my comfort zone but I ended up loving them. Michelle taught ballet and jazz and Andrea still taught my lyrical class. I grew to look up to my dance teachers. They taught me so much about not only dance but about life. They taught me perseverance and humility. They helped give me a positive outlet to let my feelings out. I felt free. I stopped cutting my body. I started demonstrating for various classes. I became a role model.

I made the competition team and performed my first solo. One of the dance moms made my costume. I didn't know what to expect. I've never performed a solo before. i'm terrified. i messed up, i'm a failure. everyone probably thinks i'm a horrible dancer. i hate myself. what are people thinking about me? are they making fun of me? negative thoughts spiraled in my brain. i took the thoughts out on myself. i restricted.

I used the studio to get away. When I was having a bad day, I looked forward to dance. My days got to the point where if I wasn't at school or the gym, I was at the studio. I always danced better when i was upset or having a bad day. I spent a lot of time with Andrea helping her assist in her classes. I got close to her. I told her some of my story. I asked her advice. She encouraged me to keep dancing and letting my emotions out. She gave me permission and I needed that. Andrea has the same sense of humor as I do and she utilized tough love to get through to me. I am stubborn as heck.

I increased my classes and added hip-hop and pointe. I took every style except for tap. I loved it. Whenever we would go to competitions, I would either ride with Andrea or Michelle and stay with Michelle in the hotel room. I was sad my mom never came to see me at a competition, but it was fun to be with my dance teachers and friends without feeling like I had to censor myself. I felt like with my mom I had to walk on eggshells because I didn't want to make anything worse since taking her husband away.

When the time came to pick the lead for the ballet, everyone was excited. There was a lot of pressure. when i didn't get picked, i felt awful about myself and told myself that it was because i was too fat. Later on, I realized that those experiences actually taught me humility. It taught me to be grateful for and excited about my dance friends. Growing up, I didn't feel grateful for other people's successes. I was too concerned about survival.

My senior year was my best year in the dance world. I felt confident. I was still comparing myself to my friends but I felt different. I felt fierce and sassy. I felt like I belonged. I loved my solo my senior year. I was able to dance my solo in show-time that year. I actually became kind of good throughout the years. Of course, I always feel like I could be better…but that's the self-criticism talking.

I am forever thankful for the lessons I was taught through dance and the people I have met. They have helped change my life and introduced me to a healthy coping skill for my toolbox. Dance became a safe space for me. My studio was my escape. The first place I truly felt safe.

Journal prompt:

Take time to do something nice for yourself.

What is your favorite hobby?

_____

_____

Do you do that hobby often? If not, what is getting
in the way?

_____

_____

When is a time this week you can make time to do your
favorite hobby?

_____

_____

What are some obstacles you could face?

_____

_____

_____

How will you work through those obstacles when they come up? Who could help you? What do you need in order for those obstacles to become less?

_____

_____

_____

CHAPTER EIGHT:

hello, ed. my silent killer.

in high school i put my worth in my grades. if i got lower than an "a" i hated myself and punished myself by working out. my value was in the percentages—the numbers. even if i had an "a," if it wasn't one hundred percent or close to it, i felt like a failure. i had to be perfect. i had to be perfect because maybe if i was, someone would love me. maybe if i was, people wouldn't be mad at me for putting my dad away. maybe if i was, my dad wouldn't hate me. maybe i wouldn't hate myself.

even if i got a one hundred, i still hated myself. there was no winning in my mind. when i would write my notes, i would write in pen because it was neater. if i made even one mistake, i had to start over. one night i was writing notes for one of my AP/honors classes and i was on the last line of the page and i messed up the word. i started crying and wrinkled the paper and started over. my mom asked why i was crying and panicking and i told her it was because i ruined my notes. i tried to explain why they were ruined but she had no idea. "you don't have to start over" mom told me. yes, i do. it has to be perfect. it brought me back to the time when i was waiting for my tv show, heroes, to come on and i missed five minutes of the show. i was crying because i couldn't start from the beginning. my dad got mad at me. even at a young age, i knew i had to be perfect. it was this weird obsession of mine that things had to start from the beginning.

i eventually found myself on "dark" twitter and other forms of social media. i was looking up pictures of thin girls to motivate me to get skinny. not realizing i was already thin, i set this unrealistic expectation for myself that would only lead to my death. i didn't know what an eating disorder was at this time but i became obsessed with the idea of being thin. i became so obsessed with being thin and perfect that my worth soon went into the numbers on the scale and my appearance. i longed to be small. small enough to hide. maybe if i could hide, bad things wouldn't happen. i looked up "skinny" meals and cut out what i considered to be "bad" foods. i followed the "thin commandments" like it was the bible. my world became numbers. every food i looked at, i only saw the caloric value. when i looked at a carrot, i only saw x amount of calories. the list only grew. growing up i was taught that less equals good and i wanted to be good. i wanted so badly to be good that i ruined relationships to hide my secret.

there's that word again. secret.

i finally had a secret that was mine. i've always had a secret until dad was taken away. for years i was a vulnerable, open book. not anymore. i finally had something i felt like belonged to me. i would play a game in my head with my mom and the catch was, she didn't know. who could eat less? who could weigh the least amount? i compared myself to my mom. she would comment on her body negatively. i did not see what she saw. if she was fat, then i must be fat. one day she told me, "i weigh more than you." a lot of things did not catch me off guard, but that comment did. did she know my game? the competitive side of me only increased. i started comparing myself to my friends, random strangers in public, pictures on the internet, friends at dance. i would tear myself apart in front of the mirror daily.

my mom didn't have a scale at home so i used one whenever i could find one. when i would go to my aunt kellie's house, my mom's boyfriend at the time, or basically anywhere i could find a scale. i finally bought a scale of my own and hid it. i weighed myself multiple times a day. when i first woke up, the scale determined my mood for the day. if the number was lower than i expected, i was allowed to eat some and didn't punish myself with extra exercise. if the number was higher than expected, i wasn't allowed to eat and had to force myself to do extra miles when i ran.

one of my therapists caught on about my eating habits and mentioned i had an eating disorder. i didn't know what she meant. i felt proud. could she see the progress i've made? my therapist at the time told me she did not specialize in eating disorders and could no longer see me. i felt betrayed. my mom mentioned eating disorder to my dance teacher. i was taken from five classes to one. i was mad at my mom. i just won a ballet scholarship and made company and now i couldn't do either. what am i supposed to do now? i have no control. i know how to fix it though…make it look like i was gaining weight and that i was "fine."

i started eating in front of people but would spit food out in a napkin so i would trick them. i lied to everyone. i worked out in my room. i snuck out to go on runs. i had to have control. mom loved working out. i would go to the gym with her. i'm going to stop there because what if you mistake this book as an instruction manual. mom didn't understand eating disorders. how was she supposed to know what i was doing? i started working out at the gym and at home. i secretly searched low caloric snacks and ate those for meals. the weight dropped.

my senior year of high school is when my eating disorder really escalated. i was back in all of my dance classes because i proved to them i was eating. if i went out with friends to go to dinner or something, i had to look up the menu ahead of time and plan. i would work out at the gym, go to dance for basically half a day, then go back to the gym on the way home. i was at my lowest weight my senior year.

people started noticing my weight loss and i was forced to eat. i was losing my control again. what am i supposed to do? i gained some weight to make others happy but i hated myself more than ever. i felt like a whale. like i was garbage because i wasn't "thin." when my brudder told me that my dad molested him as well, i felt sick to my stomach. i was supposed to protect him. i held my eating disorder close to me because i felt like that was the only thing i could control. i was angry at my dad. the first time i truly felt like i hated my dad. my brudder was my best friend. how could my dad hurt someone i love?

Journal prompt:

Have you ever felt the need to be perfect? Like you needed to fit in? What is your experience? What do you feel? How far will you go to be "perfect" or to please others?

_____

_____

_____

_____

_____

_____

_____

_____

_____

_____

_____

_____

_____

_____

_____

CHAPTER TEN:

curiosity.

During college, I started getting curious about my case. I did some research and found that I could obtain a copy of my case-file from my dad's case. I contacted the jail from my hometown and inquired about this request. The facilitators at the jail told me I had to be the individual to come and get the file and my mom could not because she was not the victim. I mentioned getting my case-file to a friend and she offered to come with me. My friend and I left campus one night and drove three and a half hours to my hometown to obtain the copy of my case. When we got there, I walked into the jail and felt super anxious. I told them my name and what I was there to get and showed them my ID. The lady on the other side of the desk handed me a thick envelope. I was shocked to see how thick my file was.

what am i getting myself into?

My friend and I met up with my mom, brudder, and cousin at Dairy Queen before we headed back to campus. There were a lot of memories at Dairy Queen. My family would meet up there about once a week. I hid my case file in the car because I was afraid of someone seeing it. I was embarrassed. Ashamed. My friend and I drove back to campus. When I got back, I was exhausted but I was so eager to read my file. what was I looking for? i think i wanted a reason. a reason why my dad did the things he did. i wanted to know what his side of the case was. what he said. how he acted. i wanted the full story— not just my side.

i pulled an all-nighter reading my file. i experienced lots of emotions. i was hurt. sad. angry. numb. i did not feel a sense of satisfaction or relief like i thought i would. reading my file made me feel worse. i wanted an answer. why?

why. why. why.

i read my case file to my roommate like it was a book. it didn't phase me. i started having ptsd symptoms again. my depression and anxiety tanked. my eating tanked. i tanked.

one night i got really drunk and started crying. i was saying, "please don't hurt me. please don't hurt me." my roommate told me that i am safe and at school. she continued to reiterate i was safe. i started saying, "i know i'm safe. i'm safe. i'm safe." i would be okay for a little bit and calm down then start freaking out again. i would say, "i'm sorry. it's my fault. it's my fault you're gone and that you're going away for so long." my roommate told me that it's not my fault and she understands that i miss him and he's my dad but what he did was not okay. i continued repeating myself and then saying, "i can help other girls from what i've been through." she told me that i needed to talk to my therapist and that i need to stop holding everything inside. she told me, "i'm glad you got drunk and spilled everything because you were holding things in."

i felt better emotionally after i let it all out.

i hid my file so i wouldn't read it anymore. when i moved, i brought it with me. i held onto it like it was my baby. it was my life in papers. they meant something to me. i felt valid. like it was all real. sometimes my past feels like a bad dream. a nightmare. it doesn't feel real. having my life on paper made me feel like i mattered. i didn't know how to live without putting my worth into something physical. i needed there to be a reason for everything.

After talking with my therapist, I realized that I will probably never get an answer to why my dad did what he did. I had to be okay with that. Sometimes I still wonder why. It's natural to want to know.

the truth is my dad probably doesn't know why he did it... at least that is what i tell myself to get by.

Journal prompt:

Write 10 self-care ideas you would be willing to try.

1. _____

_____

2. _____

_____

3. _____

_____

4. _____

_____

5. _____

_____

6. _____

_____

7. _____

_____

8. _____

_____

9.

_____

_____

10.

_____

_____

CHAPTER ELEVEN:

treatment pt. I—i'm fine.

when i moved to college, i didn't have anyone telling me what to do. i didn't have anyone forcing me to eat. i once again put my worth in my grades. i worked so hard to graduate in three years instead of four. i wanted to be an overachiever. that was how i could have control. i graduated college with a semester of grad school done as well.

I was going to school for counseling. My biggest motivation was to help others who have gone through what I have (abuse wise, I still didn't believe I had an eating disorder at this point). My senior year of college, the stress became too much and I was eagerly searching for something to control. My trauma stuff started coming up again and I went to therapy. The more the trauma stuff came up, the more I stopped eating. I want so badly for my eating disorder and my trauma to be separate, but for me, they're not. My eating disorder became bad again and I was only eating spinach leaves. I became super depressed. I was running x amount of miles each day. The weight started dropping again.

july 9, 2018

i should have started journaling two months ago when i first started treatment. i don't know why i didn't. maybe i was afraid of what i may feel or find out about myself. i was in my senior year when my eating disorder (ed) started getting pretty bad again. i didn't think i had a problem—apart of me still thinks i don't. all i could think about was food and calories. to be honest, i don't remember what i learned my senior year and that scares me. the days leading up to treatment were scary. the entire spring semester, people from my school had their eyes on me. my professor knew i needed help because she could see i was losing weight and "losing it fast" she told me. she told me she could "see the bone in my nose so prominently." i was down to x pounds which was underweight for my height, but it still wasn't enough. i wasn't sick. i didn't have a problem.

my professor and i found a treatment center that treated eating disorders and helped me fill out the application. my professor also came with me to my consultation appointment at the facility. they told me that they would not start me at intensive outpatient (iop) and that i need to start at partial hospitalization (php). they told me i was bordering php and residential. i was scared and crying. i don't know what to do and i feel like i need to lose even more weight. that's what i did.

my eating disorder got worse in april when i took a bunch of laxatives my mom gave me. i got extremely dehydrated. in order to start treatment, i needed to get medically cleared. the "campus mom" took me to my doctors' appointments that day. when i got my bloodwork done, i felt awful afterwards. i kept on coming in and out of almost losing consciousness. the "campus mom" told me that if i passed out, she was taking me straight to the hospital instead of my next appointment. she told me to eat the yogurt i brought and i was crying because i didn't want to gain the weight. during my next doctor's appointment, my ekg came back abnormal (which i never followed up on because i thought i was just dehydrated). when we were driving back to campus, the "campus mom" kept talking to me trying to keep me conscious and helped me back to my room. i ended up passing out when i got to my room and she stayed with me until i fell asleep.

after a few hours i woke up and let the "campus mom" know i was awake. i didn't realize my roommate and r.a. were in her office at the time. my r.a. texted me telling me she heard what happened and told me she was worried and asked if she could take me to the hospital. i told her "no, i'm fine." she continued to ask me and i didn't have the energy to fight anymore so i told her "fine." my r.a. and roommate rushed to my room and helped me get dressed. i passed out in my r.a.'s arms and she rushed to get her car and took me to the hospital. i passed out again in the emergency room and don't remember much else from the day. my roommate and r.a. told me i looked gray and lifeless and they thought i was going to die. they told me the hospital gave me three to four bags of fluids and had me hooked to a heart monitor. after that, i fought to make it to graduation so i could walk across the stage. that was honestly a bigger accomplishment than completing my degree. the "campus mom" told me she cried when i walked across the stage because she didn't think i was going to make it let alone walk across the stage. i started treatment a week after i graduated.

may 11, 2018

when i got to the facility, i was terrified. i didn't need treatment. i wasn't thin enough to need treatment. they probably
think i'm a joke. i had to go to treatment from noon until
seven pm. the dietitian tech showed me around the facility.
the kitchen was so overwhelming. food was in almost every
cabinet from top to bottom and the fridge was filled. i couldn't
do anything but cry. i then had to do my weigh in and vitals
check with a woman named, stacey. stacey checked my vitals
and they have a blind scale so i couldn't see my weight. that
didn't matter though because i have a scale at home.

it was lunch time and i had to go prep my lunch. i couldn't
finish it so i had to be supplemented. the first time i have ever
been supplemented for not finishing a meal. after the supplement i felt as full as someone does after a thanksgiving meal. all
i wanted to do was take a nap. we had a few groups and then
it was time for snack. i didn't want to finish my snack because
i was still full from lunch and the supplement. i finished my
snack and we went for a mindful walk. dinner was difficult. i
brought a cliff bar and they made me add onto it. i didn't finish
all of it but i had most of it. my therapist, jenn, told me i could
be done and thanked me for trying.

as the days in treatment continued, they kept getting
harder and harder. i have had to supplement more times than
i can count. i met with the dietitian and got my meal plan. i
lost weight and gained weight and lost weight again. i started
struggling a lot. i didn't care about my health. i wasn't scared
of dying. all i was concerned about was losing weight. jenn
put me on one hundred percent physical movement restric-
tion and told me that she was concerned that if i kept running,

then my heart would stop and i wouldn't come back from it. my dietitian added supplements into my meal plan and i was so upset because i felt like i was already eating more than i needed to. it was too much food. do they actually expect me to eat all of this? i'm not doing this whole recovery thing. it's too much. i told my professor about treatment and told her i don't want to go back. i started blaming it on work and telling her i couldn't keep taking off of work. she responded, "i pray that treatment is your top priority. you will get out what you put in. fully invest. <u>do not</u> let something as stupid as work at a candle store have even 1% impact on your treatment which will impact you, your family, every client you touch, and many lives that lay ahead. you got this!" she was right. i needed to put everything into my recovery. however, my eating disorder started comparing myself to the other patients there. who could be the sickest? my eating disorder hated jenn—it was afraid of her.

jenn and i talked about an emotional support animal and how it would help me with my trauma and anxiety. i asked her what all was involved and i did my research. i found a dog and jenn wrote me a letter. i picked up my eight-week-old puppy and named him maslow (after maslow's hierarchy of needs). he became my everything. he motivated me to keep going in recovery and gave me a purpose.

a couple months of treatment went by. and i went from php to iop. this is a good thing; however, my eating disorder convinced me it was not. my eating disorder came back to the forefront of my brain and i started going downhill again. i was deteriorating fast. my eating disorder got to the point where i was almost sent to residential twice. my treatment team told me that i was losing weight so rapidly that they couldn't keep up. that only fueled the fire. i have been having a really rough time getting food into my body. i thought my mindset was for recovery but for some reason, i could not force myself to eat. i was still working out outside of treatment and basically undoing everything i was doing.

july 12, 2018

treatment is horrible today. today i am supposed to have a candy bar for my challenge snack but there were no reeses and i don't like any other candy bar. i had a croissant with nutella in it. my "ed" was in full force and i was not having it. jenn was sitting across from me and she told me, "your ed is defiant right now." i told her i wasn't going to eat that. so i had a supplement (i didn't grab one like i was supposed to before snack). jenn and i sat at the table and she was talking to me about how i keep punishing myself and how i don't allow myself to enjoy things. i cried and cried. jenn teared up a few times and said during part of our conversation that it broke her heart she couldn't wish me a happy birthday on my birthday but if she did, i would have been more hurt…she kept on saying it is hard for her because i cannot see my worth and she is absolutely right. i can't.

jenn and i had a session together soon after and it was the first time i have been one hundred percent honest without holding anything bad because i was afraid of judgement. we talked about how the part of me that misses my dad is holding onto the eating disorder. she explained to me that i have been punished my whole life and now that my dad is not around, i am punishing myself. she was right. i didn't want to believe her but it was true. jenn mentioned that i have been in sur-vival mode and surviving my entire life and it is time for me to thrive.

i became super motivated and thought there was only two labels i had—victim and survivor. i didn't know i could thrive. i thought life stopped at surviving. i never realized there was more to life than surviving until my conversation with jenn. i don't want to stay a survivor. i want to thrive in my life. jenn asked me where the thirteen-year-old me was. the thir-teen-year-old me who fought and stood up to my dad.

i keep punishing and torturing myself because i want to hold onto my dad. the fact is that by trying to hold onto my dad, he is still having control over my life. every time i eat, i am taking my life back. i want to start thriving because i'm not a victim anymore. i'm not just a survivor anymore.

jenn really hyped me up. she was the best therapist i've had thus far and didn't let me get away with shit. she showed me tough love but that's what i needed. jenn, stacey, and trish (my first dietitian) believed in me since i started. they believed in me when i didn't believe in myself. i brought my scale into treat-ment one day which was a big move for me. i gave my scale to stacey and jenn #recoverywin. i was excited but super anxious. the scale was my best friend and my worst enemy. during one of the groups, we wrote eulogies and had a "funeral" for our scales. we broke our scales and then buried them. jenn kept getting after me because i wasn't acting like i wanted my scale to die because i was hitting it like a "wimp." a part of me didn't. but a bigger part of me knew it was the right thing to do. here is my eulogy to my scale and my eating disorder:

my dearest scale,

it feels strange to address you in such formal terms—after all, we are old friends. i remember when we first met. when you reassured me that everything was going to be okay. you introduced yourself to me back in elementary school. you comforted me when dad called me fat and that i was built like a man. you told me that you knew how to make it all go away. you became my security blanket. it started out with innocent "healthy eating" until it was overtaken by your authoritarian control. you categorized my small frame as "too big" and told me that if i followed your rules, then i would be pretty and worth loving.

i was naive and believed you. you weren't my friend anymore—you became a dictator. you manipulated me. you blinded me. you determined my daily thoughts. they consisted of what i could eat that day, what my mood was, how i would get out of dinner plans with family/friends, and when i could next weigh myself. when i found myself obsessing over food, calories, and over exercising, i knew that i was in for it. i was obsessed with you.

i started lying to those who i loved the most. saying "i'm not hungry," "i already ate," or "i don't feel well." you completely isolated me within your world of lies, rules and paranoia. eventually i couldn't distinguish your voice from my own. you taught me how to crave hunger. even the thought of death didn't fill me with fear. losing weight became an accomplishment and starvation became a game we would play. "how long can you go this week without eating" you would say.

there were times i could get away from you. actually enjoy life and eat what i want; however, you would always find a way back into my life when i stepped back on you. i lost joy in the things that once made me happy. i started using my healthy outlets of dance and running as a way for me to lose weight. my hair started to fall out, i stopped getting my periods, i barely had the energy to get out of bed, and my skin was as pale as a ghost, but you told me the bones protruding from my skin were beautiful, and that kept me going. despite being too weak to walk up the stairs without seeing spots, i had never felt stronger.

you told me my worth was dependent by the number read on the scale. that my worth was measured by the amount of calories i put into my body as if it were a sin. but how ridiculous does that sound? no matter what or how much i eat and weigh will ever prove how great of a daughter, sister or friend i am. i am slowly realizing i am beautiful inside and out. the ugly part of me has always been you.

i now see the blunt reality, the truth you sheltered me from for so long. there is no end goal, no golden promise. no matter how much weight i lose, it will never be good enough for you. my story has a happy ending and it's time to quit pretending. i have a different view and it's one that doesn't include you.

sincerely,
-megs

For so long I found my identity in either the eating disorder or what my dad did to me. I was talking to Missy, one of the other therapists on my current treatment team, one day and told her that I could finally make Meghan be who I want her to be and who she deserve to be. I have never been at a healthy adult weight and I realize that numbers don't matter anymore. I'm starting to nourish my body and because of that, my body will naturally go to its set point. I can sacrifice a few months of discomfort for a lifetime of happiness without the disorder or my past following me. I am worth more than being punished and tortured for something I had no control over. I am worth more than pain and suffering. I am worth more than a number on a scale. I am not my past. I found my worth. I found my fight.

i wish i could say that recovery was super easy from here on out but if i did, i would be lying to you. i would be lying to you and i am here to be real with you. i feel like recovery became harder. now that i chose recovery, i had to keep choosing recovery every day. choosing recovery is not a one time deal, unfortunately.

my treatment team decided i needed to come to treatment on saturdays too because my weight was still declining. i remember my friend monty and i were the only ones there one saturday. we were making pizza bagels, and both had a panic attack. we were freaking out about the carbs in the bagel. we got through it by eating together—one bite at a time. we encouraged each other. i was talking to the therapist that was there that saturday and was crying. we were talking about my past and i allowed her to hug me. this was a big step for me because i wouldn't let anyone touch me. it was a proud moment for both of us.

some of my other friends in treatment, ash and zoe, also helped motivate me at times. ash, zoe, monty, and i became a pack. we started a group chat called, "ed slayers." we used it to support and encourage each other. we still use this group chat today. i remember when i first started treatment and ash was my first friend there. we were very similar. we both anxiously laughed and had crippling anxiety. jenn encouraged me to try anxiety medication and it has been a lifesaver. i always refused to take medication because i didn't want to gain weight from it but i trusted jenn so i gave it a try. when i first met zoe, she was the sweetest girl. i didn't even know her and she made me a birthday card because i was in treatment on my birthday. she has a hippy vibe and i love it. monty introduced me to some rad music. treatment was hard but sometimes it was fun.

one day when i got to treatment and stacey took my vitals, i went to get snack. jenn and my dietitian pulled me into an office and told me that my vitals were bad. they wanted to send me to the hospital. i begged them not to. they told me i had to eat my snack and a supplement right now. i did. i hated every second of it but i did it. each morning when stacey took my vitals, we would talk. we found we had a lot in common. we became close. she was one of the reasons i tried so hard. at the time i had to choose recovery for others and not myself because i couldn't trust myself. i still saw myself as bad but i was working on it. that is what mattered.

july 19, 2018

i keep thinking of when i was at an orthostatic number of over x and jenn almost sent me to res and was weighing me every day. when they had me go to treatment on saturdays too. i was going through my things and found some letters i wrote to my dad when i was thirteen and i got so triggered. i need to get rid of them as soon as possible but i can't. i have no idea what to think or feel right now. i feel numb and so conflicted. i'm going to bring the letters to treatment and maybe share them. i just need to get them out of my possession...i honestly don't know what i want. i want to stay sick—it's my comfort. at the same time though, i have my entire life ahead of me. during my session with jenn, she told me that if i tank again, she is putting me back up to php. she also asked me when i am going to stop punishing myself. i honestly don't know if i can stop. during dinner i was crying because i felt like i needed to punish myself and restrict. one of the therapists asked me what was going on and i told her what i was feeling and why. she wiped my tears. it was a little weird, but it was the first time i actually let my treatment team care for me.

i gave the letters to jenn to hold onto until i gathered the strength to shred them.

august 9, 2018

i got discharged from treatment. my dietitian told me i shouldn't' be discharged and that i should be baker acted. she told me that by me moving, i am going against her medical advice. my therapist cried a lot. she told me i went past her boundaries which is very hard to do. she told me that she along with the rest of my treatment team is so scared and she cried. she told me she doesn't want me to be her first client to die...i don't want to start with a new therapist and dietitian. i'm not about to start all over again. i don't want to gain weight. my "healthy" weight is too much and i feel like everyone just wants me to get fat.

i went against my treatment team's advice and moved anyway.

Journal prompt:

Stop. Have you eaten today?
If not, grab a snack and let's eat together.

What did you pick?

_____

That sounds yummy!! How does it taste? What are the flavors
you are experiencing? What is the texture?

_____

_____

_____

_____

_____

_____

What are your thoughts and feelings?

_____

_____

_____

_____

Are you done? Great job! I know it's not easy. Your body thanks you for fueling it and giving it energy. Food is fuel. Food is medicine.

CHAPTER TWELVE:
the big move.

My brudder drove with me when I moved to Tennessee. When leaving Florida, we visited my treatment facility so that I could say bye. Jenn gave me some supplements and made sure to tell my brudder to make sure I drink them. My brudder cared a lot about me and made sure I ate and drank the supplements. I got mad at him and took my anger out on him. He put up with me. We stopped in Georgia for the night to get some sleep with Maslow. The next day we made it to Tennessee.

i was super emotional the entire trip because i was moving away from all of my friends and family to somewhere where i had no support. my main focus was grad school. i just wanted to keep pushing myself and was determined to finish school so that i could help other people. my brudder helped me move and buy things for my apartment. he helped me get groceries. i continued to email jenn and stacey for support. i had no idea what i was getting myself into.

before i left florida, jenn set me up with an appointment with an eating disorder facility in the town i was moving to so that i could continue getting therapy and have a dietitian. the day after i moved up to tennessee was my appointment. i went to the facility by myself after i dropped my brudder off at the airport and was terrified. i didn't want to start over. i wanted to stick with jenn. i begged jenn to keep seeing me virtually but she couldn't due to ethical laws.

i walked into the facility and checked in at the front desk. the facility seemed cozy. the front desk staff was nice. i was hateful. i sat on the couch in the waiting room and sunk down until the staff called my name to come back. i saw the dietitian, lisa, for half of a session and a therapist for the other half. lisa took me back to get my weight and i felt embarrassed. embarrassed because she had to see me weighing as much as i did—not because i was underweight but because i saw myself as severely overweight. during the sessions i barely talked. i decided during the sessions i did not want to start over and i was not going to continue treatment. i didn't need help. i just needed to focus on myself. i knew what was best for me. no one knows my body better than i do. i went back home and fell back into my eating disorder full force. i started grad school but then decided it was too much at the time and deferred a semester. i started my new job working in a crisis setting and loved it. my boss, sarah, hired me when i was still in florida. we had a phone interview and i was excited when i got the position because that meant i had a job when i moved. i also had a job in the field i loved so that was a plus.

i was still struggling with my eating disorder but was trying to keep it a secret because i didn't want anyone to know. sarah pulled me into an office one day and told me that when she was contacting my references, someone told her about my eating disorder, and she felt weird knowing about it and i didn't know she knew. i felt super vulnerable. am i going to get fired? i didn't want anyone to know. i wanted to start fresh. sarah knowing about my "ed" is keeping me accountable because i don't want her to think i can't do my job.

i was still running and over exercising. i was still restricting. sarah told me i could keep boosts and my food in the fridge in her office. i got in to see a new therapist when my insurance kicked in three months after i moved to tennessee. i didn't get along with her. when i first moved, trish saw me until i got in with a dietitian up here. as the holidays came around and i was in a new state by myself, my mental health deteriorated. i stopped eating, started lying to sarah about my boosts. i would take my boosts out of her fridge and put them in my locker so she thought i drank them. i lied to my dietitian, my therapist, and all my friends and family.

november 4, 2018

sarah had a very direct conversation with me today about my "ed" and my job. i was genuinely scared i was going to lose my job. i've been trying so hard ever since the conversation but the less i focus on my eating disorder, the more my trauma comes up—i'm not about to deal with that right now... sarah and i talked about art and she introduced me to an artist i fell in love with. i started having snacks in sarah's office at work which helped me because i had accountability. i feel bad though because helping me eat is not her job...

i started dropping weight. when i over exercised, i would pass out but continue to push myself over my limits. i started taking an excessive amount of laxatives. my doctors became concerned and had me getting lab work twice a week because my levels changed so rapidly. i was in the hospital because of my heart and the x amount of laxatives i took. my heart was failing. my kidneys were failing. my liver was failing. i was dying. i didn't have any energy to let maslow outside and he would go to the bathroom in the apartment. i didn't have energy to do my job efficiently. sarah was afraid i was going to die.

december 20, 2018

yesterday i had my dietitian appointment. she told me my weight is going in the wrong direction and it is declining. she told me there is no negotiation and that i need to eat. she told me i am going to be in residential if i keep going the way i am going. sarah told me i am jeopardizing my job and my insurance. i honestly don't know what to do. i can't get myself to eat. all of my safe foods are fear foods again. i can't go to treatment because then i'll lose my job and insurance. i don't know what to do. i don't want to recover. i want people to leave me alone honestly. sarah told me she was worried the other day. i feel so bad. i'm trying to cover my body so people can't see the weight loss. i'm trying to think of ways to fake gaining weight so that my dietitian won't know. sarah told me the other day, "just know people do care if you succeed." i really don't care about my life. i hate myself so much. i don't deserve to recover. i don't deserve friends. i don't deserve to be cared for. i think in a way i want the "ed" to kill me. i have no value to my life. i'm not even skinny. i was hoping my size x jeans would be a little bit loose but they feel normal. i need to just pretend like nothing ever happened and stop talking about my eating. i hate myself for not going to residential when i had the chance.

my dietitian at the time told me she could no longer see me and i needed a higher level of care. i didn't understand. i was "fine." she fired me and referred me to iop. i went to do the assessment to get into iop and realized it was the same facility i had attempted to try when i first moved. i went into the office and sat down. not even five minutes into the assessment, the lady doing it told me, "i'm recommending you to residential." i became angry and upset. i begged her to at least finish the assessment before they made any decisions because i couldn't go to residential (res). she responded with, "we can finish the assessment but that's still going to be my recommendation." i tried changing my answers to the questions so she would change her mind about res thinking that would help. i attempted to waterload so that i could falsify my weight and hope that would be enough to keep me from going inpatient. everyone was telling me i need residential, even my doctor.

january 17, 2019

i woke up and was super exhausted. i didn't want to go to any of my appointments. i had my dietitian appointment first and when she weighed me, she didn't tell me if i gained or lost but seemed upset. she pulled out a granola bar and wouldn't let me leave until i finished it all and i was already so full. she told me i was pale and need residential. afterwards i had my therapy appointment. my therapist told me my hands and face were pale and he was afraid i was going to die before i even made it to get treatment. i feel like a failure. i'm letting everyone down.

january 19, 2019

yesterday the treatment center where i did my assessment with called me and told me i have to go to residential and they won't start me at anything lower because i need to be medically monitored. she told me that the director, clinicians, dietitian, and medical team looked over my labs and are all concerned and agreed it wouldn't be safe for me to start at any level lower than residential. i'm so upset and terrified.

mostly because i don't want to gain weight. i talked to sarah and cried and cried and she talked to her boss. her boss came to tell me herself that they are going to hold my position at work, and they are all rooting for me and want me to get better. the treatment team wanted me to start res today but i need to get everything situated. they said normally they don't admit on a friday, but they will admit me...i'm so terrified for treatment. i know this is what i need but my anxiety has been through the roof. i'm nervous to work on myself. i don't know who i am without the eating disorder. i'm afraid to lose it. i feel like i'm letting everyone down. sarah told me that i'd be letting people down if i didn't receive treatment.

monday comes around and on january 21, i drove to residential.

Meditation prompt:

Close your eyes if you feel safe enough to do so and notice your breath. Focus on the inhales and exhales without trying to control it. Starting from your toes and going up your body, thank each body part for what it does for you throughout the day. When negative thoughts come, notice them and dismiss them. Keep breathing.

CHAPTER THIRTEEN:

treatment pt. II— knocking on death's door.

as i am driving to residential, a lot of doubt comes up. am i doing the right thing? am i even sick enough to have to go to residential? everyone there is going to think i'm a joke. i'm too fat to be going to residential. i haven't eaten anything yet. if i'm gonna go, i'm going to go in empty. as i am approaching the facility, i stop at taco bell to go to the bathroom because the laxatives i took that morning were starting to hit me. i walk in to the facility and meet with a girl named ashley and told her, "i am supposed to be starting residential today and i'm here and don't know what i'm doing." she told me to bring my bags and drop them off at the front desk and then come in her office. i get to her office and my anxiety is through the roof. i'm joking around with her because that's how i deal with my anxious thoughts. she takes my picture. the entire time i am thinking i am too fat to be here. i am super self-conscious of my picture and everything about myself. she asked what i ate today. "nothing" i replied. "oh, so you're coming to us empty, are you?" yes. yes, i was. i had to use the last bit of control i had before it was taken away from me.

i felt like i hit rock bottom. like there's no way to go but up from here. sarah told me she had to come to terms with my death. was i really dying? was it really that bad?

january 21, 2019

ashley brought me onto the eating disorder unit and i got my vitals checked. i met with the nurse, aleisha, and she admitted me to the unit. the techs brought me to get my snack and there was already a menu slip that was highlighted by the dietitian: a fruit, cheese stick, and crackers.

i don't know why i have to have three things. i grabbed an apple and crackers but i only ate the apple. i told the tech that i would save the crackers for later but i can't eat the crackers and the cheese stick. she told me that usually when i don't finish, i would have to have a supplement but they're lenient my first day (which the eating disorder is taking full advantage of). after snack the group went on a grocery outing but i couldn't go because i can't go on any outings for five days—something about medical clearance. i keep comparing myself to the other girls here. i ended up having to have a supplement for night snack because i didn't have the cheese stick and i was so mad at myself because the cheese stick had less calories. i'm so dumb. i need to work out in my room before my shower.

the first night i didn't have a roommate which was nice. the next morning the nurse woke me up super early for weigh in. the weigh ins are random and i hate that because i can't be sneaky and make it look like i gained more weight. they also weigh us in gowns. i was super uncomfortable. when we go to the bathroom, someone has to check before we can flush to make sure we didn't use any behaviors. it took me eight weeks to poop in front of one of the techs—sorry whitney. i journaled everyday i was in residential. i wanted to document this journey so that i could look back and see how far i come. i filled two journals during my time in res.

my second night, i had to sleep in the group room to have accountability not to exercise since i still did not have a roommate. a part of me was grateful and felt relieved i didn't have to exercise. the eating disorder part of me was very pissed off. pissed off because i couldn't compensate for eating that day— especially after the supplements. i hate myself so much. why am i even here?

january 23, 2019

my stomach hurts so bad. i want to exercise but i am trying to remember why i am here and give it one hundred and ten percent like i told everyone i would. we did a yoga group this morning and a dance movement group. i love the movement groups. in the group, my butt bones hurt so bad because they kept rubbing against the chair. the same thing happens at the table. one of the other patients gave me a cushion to use during groups and at the table. that was really nice of her. the patients are super nice but i'm still scared to talk to them. i had to pee in a cup again because there is still blood in my urine, so they are keeping an eye on it. the dance movement group and yoga group were so good today. i felt motivated for recovery. after the groups though i immediately started telling myself i was gaining too much weight and how fat i was. i have to keep reminding myself that i am here to recover and i don't want to keep dealing with this. i also keep telling myself that i'm on a different journey than other people here. yes, we are all here for recovery, but each person's recovery is different. i need to start changing my thoughts about my body and i am trying to be more conscious about that. it helps that i have so much time on my hands to work on myself. during one of the groups the new admit was talking about acknowledging the eating disorder (ed) thoughts/urges/behaviors but then also going deeper and thinking about <u>why</u> you are engaging in ed behaviors.

i've been having urges to exercise so i tried thinking about why i am having those urges. i discovered that i am having those urges because i feel like i am losing control and being forced to gain weight but then i realized i do have control because i am controlling my own recovery. i have been through so much and owe it to myself and deserve recovery. my dietitian, addie, pulled me for session during the art therapy group. during our session we went over my menus and meal plan. my meal plan is smaller which helps because i still have no hunger cues and my stomach hurts so bad. apparently, they have to refeed me. i'm also extremely constipated which isn't fun. addie was nice. i like her better than my outpatient dietitian i was seeing before residential. addie and i were talking about carbs and she explained to me that i would eat five apples but freak out over one slice of bread. she told me that apples are a carbohydrate like bread is. she told me that our bodies don't understand what an apple is or a slice of bread is. our bodies just see a carbohydrate and digests it—turn it into glucose and energy for our brain. i tried remembering that during dinner tonight because i had pasta. i finished it though. #recoverywin.

one of the other patients, lof (loaf) and i had a really good talk tonight. i felt connected and motivated. the girls here are super supportive, don't compare their meals and tries their hardest to finish all their meals and snacks. this helps motivate me. the other girls here also challenge themselves. i was talking to lof and telling her that when i get out, i want to be able to eat without having crippling anxiety. i want to be able to eat what i want when i want. i want to learn how to listen to my body and give her what she needs. i want to fall in love with her and respect her because she deserves it and is worth it.

during yoga today we did this tapping exercise and during it i kept telling myself that my body is a safe place. i am hoping to one day believe it. i have a very different mindset this round of treatment. like i actually want to recover. i was trying so hard to stay out of residential but honestly, this is where i need to be right now. i realized that if i'm not recovering, i'm dying.

january 24, 2019

here is one of the journal prompts we did today: i am. journal about the ways in which you find yourself performing to demonstrate your own value.

my need for perfection came from the abuse. i would try to be the perfect child because maybe i wouldn't get raped or hit that day. i think it also came from my need for control. i didn't have any control growing up and so i started making everything perfect because i could control that. i also wanted to make everyone else happy and please others. i find my value is to make sure others are happy even when i'm not. i'm trying to change that though because i'm slowly learning that i also deserve to be happy. i feel like it would feel _amazing_ to let go of performance and embrace authenticity. it feels comforting to know that it is okay to not be perfect. i think it is so important to be real and authentic because i feel like i can connect more to others and feel like i am not being fake or hiding anything. i feel free when i'm being authentic which is a foreign concept and makes me feel super uncomfortable but i am trying to sit with the uncomfortableness feeling because i do deserve to be free and live a happy life. i am worth it. i am resilient. i am compassionate. i am strong. i am fearless...

...we answered questions from the internal family systems guide to healing part by part book.

1.when reading this chapter, i noticed a submissive, quiet, scared, little girl. i noticed six-year-old me.

2.there is a part of me who feels like i'll never be able to recover. this part of me is the six-year-old me who is hiding. she is hopeless, scared, sad, tired, and anxious.

3. there is a part of me who feels like i want to get better. this part of me is the adult version of me (older than i am now). she's compassionate, hopeful, happy, motivated, and trying to take care of the six-year-old me who won't let her in.

4. i do feel empty inside. my reaction to the emptiness thoughts are depression, numbness, and self-hatred.

5. when thinking about my own recovery, i have been focusing on the eating, food, and weight. my recovery has felt like it's going nowhere. this time around in residential, i am trying to focus on finding peace with myself first which has been overwhelming.

6.when in recovery, i envision i will be genuinely happy. i wouldn't isolate myself so much and i won't be as anxious around food. i will feel more content with myself and find self-love for my body. there may be more but when those things happen, i will know i have achieved self-acceptance and peace. also, when the little girl inside of me feels safe.

i'm still having to take caffeine supplements to detox and mirolax because i'm constipated. when they do weigh in day, i feel like the nurses, techs, addie, and whoever else sees my weight is going to judge me. i feel like i'm gaining too much.

january 27, 2019

last night when i went to check in with the nurse, i told her everything from the better off dead feelings i've been having to the exercise i did. she told me to sleep in the day room last night so i did.

my vitals were a little abnormal this morning, but it was fine. i went to the nurse to get my meds and feel better than i did last night. i am super exhausted but it was nice to have accountability. this week i am really focusing on challenging myself more. i think tomorrow i'm going to talk to addie because i'm getting hungry and that scares me because i'm afraid she's going to increase my nutrient number. the "ed" is going crazy because a part of me genuinely wants to take advantage and not say anything so that i can lose weight. i talked to lof about it and she told me to be honest with addie and tell her. she is right. if i don't tell her, i'm just going to make myself go backwards and undo all the hard work i am doing. i am not going to let the "ed" have that control. i'm here to recover. i'm so tired of having my life on pause and just want to move on and recover from this. i think i'm going to tell addie i was also thinking of not finishing my night snack so i could have a supplement to help fill me up. lof told me that my body is trying to tell me what it needs and i need to take care of her. she doesn't have to be punished anymore. dad isn't here to hurt me anymore and i need to stop hurting and punishing myself because i honestly don't deserve it.

i hope one day i can truly believe that i don't deserve to be punished.

february 2, 2019

last night, it was freezing in my room so cassie, one of the nurses, brought in a space heater from the nurse's station. she's honestly the sweetest. after breakfast we put on the barbie swan lake movie until it was time to go to process group. process group was <u>so</u> insightful today and i'm still in awe and my mind is still blown.

THE MOUNTAIN TOP

we did an exercise during one of the process groups that led to my breakthrough in my recovery/healing journey. we were encouraged to think of a safe, calming, place. a place where we felt at peace. for years when i would try to meditate, i would visualize myself on the edge of a mountain top, staring off into the mountains. i could not ever see what was behind me on the visualized mountain top until the morning of february 2, 2019.

i am sitting in one of the group rooms at my treatment center in the same seat as i always do—the burgundy chair in the left corner with the dim light behind me. after our check in where we voice how we feel physically and emotionally, we started the meditation exercise. i closed my eyes and began to think of a mountain top cliff. i am sitting on the edge with my legs crossed, hair up in a messy bun (my go to hairstyle), and looking out beyond the mountains. in the visualization i am the same age i am now, twenty-one. the sky is blue, there is a nice breeze on my face; blowing the baby hairs around, and fog among the tips of the mountains. the therapist then encourages us to think of our advisor. i am confused and began to become frustrated with myself because i could not think of an advisor. i thought of my biological father, "j," and felt a disturbance within my body—clearly, he was not the advisor.

i thought of God and couldn't bring myself to think of Him as the advisor in the moment because i was angry with him. i became so annoyed with myself that i gave up and just continued trying to follow along with the meditation exercise as best i could.

the therapist then encourages us to think of a path leading to a calm place. again, i could not see a path or anything the therapist was encouraging us to visualize. here i am continuing to look and look for a freaking path that did not exist in my mind. suddenly, i visualized myself turning around on the mountain top. as i turned around, i saw woods and a plethora of trees that looked uninviting. the sky over the woods on the mountain top turned a dark, gloomy, gray color and the air became chilly. as i continued looking around, i saw a cardboard box on the path in front of the terrifying woods. the cardboard box is cracked open and has dents everywhere on it like someone beat it with a baseball bat. i spoke to the cardboard box and said, "hello? if anyone is in there, you can come out now. it is safe."

next thing i know, a younger version of myself crawls out of the box. she is about 3 years old. the little girl barely comes out of the box and she is holding a worn out, dirty teddy bear. the little girl is in a dirty, pink, spaghetti strapped nightgown with dirt and bruises all over her body. her hair looks like it hasn't been brushed in years. at that moment, i realized that older me was younger me's advisor. i was wearing a t-shirt, sweatpants, and my hair still up in a messy bun. the advisor (older me) tells the little girl, "thank you for trusting me enough to come out of your box. i am not going to come any closer unless you invite me to. it is your choice. you don't have to talk or even listen to what i have to say. are you open to hearing what i want to share with you?" the little girl gently nods her head yes. the advisor continues, "my sweet girl, you are safe now. your body is safe. i am not going to let anything bad happen to you again. if you ever need me, i am

going to be right here looking at the beautiful world. i under-
stand you aren't able to see how beautiful the world is right now
but one day you will. if you need me, just open up the box and i
will turn around. i will not come closer to you until you invite
me to do so." the little girl then crawled back into her box and
locked herself in. the advisor turned around and looked back
towards the mountains.

after i processed it all, I realized that the advisor has always
been older me and the little girl who ran off and hid when my
abuse started didn't feel safe enough to come out of her box. there-
fore, she did not ever let me see her. now that my body and mind
is ready to process the trauma after nine years, the little girl came
out. this is why this is the first time I have ever seen her in my life.

my mind is so blown. when the little girl was showing up,
my body physically felt tense so i had to ground myself with
my grounding rock and it brought me back to the advisor.

during the understanding ed group, we talked about abusive relationships and it brought up a lot of stuff from my past
but i kept trying to use the grounding rock. i would catch
myself disassociating and i could come back. i didn't ever disassociate completely. i have never done that before.

i got a glimpse of the little girl fighting and screaming in
her box and it was shaking and moving all around. she did not
call out for help. the advisor (me) didn't go help her because she
didn't want to break that trust, but her heart hurt.

my body physically felt tense and like i was being abused
again. it was the weirdest thing i have ever felt. after lunch,
my therapist pulled me, and we had a family session with my
mom. it was really hard for me. a lot of stuff came up for me
that i didn't realize i was feeling. i realized i was trying to put

the family back together because i feel like i tore it apart. i kept myself so busy growing up because it was my way of continuing to survive after the abuse so i wouldn't think of memories. also, when mom called me her little girl during session, i broke down because it reminded me that i was never able to have that little girl experience and i never will. it reminded me of how i had to grow up so fast and basically had to be "okay" for the rest of my life.

during yoga, the little girl came out. i was in her eyes and she slowly unlocked the cardboard box. the little girl was looking at me through the crack of the box. her eyes were watering. she was scared to come out. when my body was completely relaxed, she slowly opened her doors. i turned around as she crawled out of her box and sat there with one leg bent up so she could hide behind it. the advisor said, "hello, i see you have opened your box. i want you to know it is safe here. are you open for listening or talking?" the little girl shook her head yes slowly. the advisor asked, "may i tell you my name?" the little girl slowly shook her head yes. "my name is meghan, but you could call me megs if you prefer. call me whatever you want. the choice is yours." the little girl sat there staring at the advisor. "i know you're scared, and you have every right to be. your feelings are valid" spoke the advisor. the little girl continued to stare.

"is there anything you need or would like from me today?" the little girl shook her head gently, yes. she took a deep breath in. the advisor spoke in her soft, slow, soothing voice; "it's okay. whatever you need, i am here. you are safe. i am not going to hurt you. i know those words don't mean anything right now. take your time. i am not going to leave you." the little girl took another deep breath. the advisor asked, "do you need me to color?" the

little girl shook her head no. "do you need a hug?" she shook her head no again and breathed deeply. "do you need me to take deep breaths?" the little girl shrugged. "hmm. do you need me to relax and be calm today?" the little nodded her head yes. "do you like it when it's calm?" she shook her head yes again. "i bet it's scary huh? i will be calm today or at least do the best i can okay? thank you for coming out to meet me today. you can stay out, go back in your box, or do something else. the choice is yours." the little girl crawled back in her box and stared at the advisor. "it's okay" the advisor said with a soft smile. the little girl closed her box and locked herself back inside. the advisor turned back around and waited patiently for the little girl to invite her again.

yoga was very different today. i felt calm and at peace. there were tears, but they were good/happy tears. after snack and group, i had a session with the dance therapist, lauren, who is also trained in emdr. we are going to start emdr next week. i am a little nervous . addie pulled me aside after lunch and told me she's going to meet with me tomorrow, but my meal plan is going to increase so she is going to add a supplement to it. i am so frustrated because my meal plan was already increased this week. why does it have to keep going up?

february 7, 2019

i'm so annoyed because i keep waking up wet from night sweats. i started spotting last night so i think i'm going to start my period. i haven't had my period in a while. i'm so upset. it's a good thing but that means i'm gaining weight. but i guess that's what i'm here to do because i need it. we did a journal prompt about what fears are keeping us from our goals:

i think fear keeps me from doing a lot of things i want to do. i have a dream to one day talk in front of a bunch of people and share my story but i'm afraid of what people would say and think. i don't like when all the attention is on me—especially when it's about my past because i don't want people to feel bad. i have goals to help victims of abuse but i need to stop letting my dad have control of me first. on the other side of fear is happiness, confidence, freedom, love, excitement, and adventure. i can see it and one day i'll be able to reach it. i know i can! one day i also want to write a book. i want the title to be called, "from victim to victory."

i'm having therapy three times a week now. it's been a lot of feelings. after dinner, four of us iced the cupcakes for night snack. i'm off of exercise precaution so i no longer have to stay in the dayroom until eleven pm. i can actually go to bed early now. for night snack, we had the cupcakes. i ate it regularly and without a fork.

my little girl wanted it and it was an opportunity for me to honor her and once i saw the blue icing i had to eat it normally like a kid would. it was honestly the best cupcake i've had. the cupcake reminded me of a little kid's birthday party.

i'm learning that it's okay to mess up. it's okay to not be perfect. there is more to life than rigid rules, pain, and suffering. i am starting to get frustrated because i can still see my chest bones and i am trying so hard in recovery. i didn't realize how much damage i've done to my body.

in treatment we had to write a letter from "ed"—here's mine:

my dearest megs,

i'm confused as to why you keep trying to get rid of me. you know you can't live without me. i've been with you for as long as you can remember. i protected you, i gave you security, a safe place, i've always been there for you. this is what you do to me? try to get rid of me? how fucking selfish of you. let me remind you of why you need me. hopefully i'll be able to knock some sense and intelligence into that shitty little brain of yours. when all those men were hurting you, who was always there for you? that's right, me. i protected you by making your mind so consumed with calories, food, exercise, the list could go on and on. i did this for you so you wouldn't get hurt anymore. i would never hurt you. i was the only constant thing in your life and i will always be the only constant thing. i only started punishing you so you would feel safe because you've never known anything different. you disappointed me when you went behind my back trying to get rid of me. in fact, you can never do anything right. you're a burden. a whore—i mean, who sleeps with all those men at such a young age? you're pathetic and a disgusting piece of shit. no one will ever love you. if someone tells you they love you, will always be there for you, will never hurt you, and that you're beautiful; don't ever believe them. you are only to believe me. only i can protect you and never hurt you. everyone else is lying. believe me when i say this—your only purpose in this life is to suffer. your weight and body disgusts everyone, even me. you will never be good enough. you deserve to be in a body bag at the bottom of a landfill. most likely a few body bags sewn together because you're so fat. you wouldn't be able to fit your goddamn leg in one of them. i can't even look at you. you know, you didn't even try to consult with me first. i thought we were closer than that. i told you you're a coward. you just proved it to yourself. all those people were right. you're a fucking piece of property with no worth. i find worth in you. i'm the only one who ever will. just keep turning to me and i'll make everything okay and safe again. the more weight you lose, the closer you are to being able to hide. to be invisible. no one will be able to hurt you then. the more you engage in behaviors, the happier i'll be and the more control you will have. you want me to be happy, don't you? after all i've done for you! just keep listening to me. don't ever try to get rid of me again.

with love,
your security blanket,
ed.

as i'm reading this letter now, after res, i see how mean my eating disorder was to me. i'm thinking now like who the fuck are you talking to? don't ever treat me like that. the letter my "ed" wrote is all lies.

february 8, 2019

during body performance group, we did an exercise where we could move to our feelings or be still.

i just felt like i needed to be still. i got a mat and sat behind a chair crisscrossed. when we were in a circle, i could see the little girl trying to unlock her box from the inside at this point, i was seeing through the little girl's eyes. when i went and sat on the mat, i went straight to the mountain top scene. the little girl crawled out and stood up. there was a sunset and the sky was orange with a hint of red, yellow, and white. the advisor turned around and stayed seated. the little girl and the advisor locked eyes. as their eyes locked, the little girl's eyes filled with tears. she stood there looking into the advisor's eyes holding her beat up teddy bear in one hand and grabbing her dirty, ripped, pink nightgown in the other.

"hello" said the advisor.

the little girl spoke for the first time. she gently trembled with a quivering lip, "hi."

"i can sense you are feeling scared and sad. do you feel sad?"

the little girl begins to cry softly as she slowly nods her head yes and clenches onto her teddy bear.

"are you feeling scared?"

the little girl responds with a gentle "yea" as tears weld then fall down her beat up face.

"are you open to talking about it?"

the little girl looked up at the advisor, sobs, and says, "i miss daddy."

"thank you for being willing to tell me. it's okay to feel sad and to miss your daddy. i miss my daddy too sometimes. why do you feel scared?"

"because sometimes i get mad at him."

"your feelings are real. it's okay to feel two feelings at once. i bet that's scary though, huh?"

the little girl slowly nods her head yes.

"is there anything i can do to help you?"

the little girl shrugged and responded, "i don't know" in her soft, innocent, three-year-old voice.

i heard the bell ding and knew it was time to start coming back to the circle. before we did the exercise, i felt sad, confusion, anger, and fear. i missed my dad and couldn't figure out why all of a sudden, out of nowhere, i missed him. i couldn't figure out if something triggered it. i didn't think anything of it. all i knew is that i missed my dad. looking back now, it was the little girl inside i found. after that group, i felt a sense of calm (even though i was sobbing). usually i have a hard time eating after something involving my dad but i didn't have a hard time. i don't feel like i miss him anymore. i don't feel sad or scared anymore.

i still can't get over the little girl talking to me. i thought it would be longer before she would do that. when i left the mountain top, the advisor was still sitting facing the little girl. the little girl was still standing after she told the advisor, "i don't know." i'm so curious as to what is going to happen. i keep thinking i am just making all of this up but every time i try to go back to it, i can't. like i'll be able to go back but i can't stay there. i can only see the last thing that happened. the last thing the little girl wanted me to see.

during the spirituality group with one of the therapists, we walked down the trail in the cold.

during the walk there was a brisk wind and it brought me back to the mountain top. the advisor and little girl were in the same position.

"are you cold?" the advisor asked.

the little girl shook her head yes.

"i have a blankie, would you like it?"

"what do i have to do for it?"

"honey, you don't have to do anything for it. you are a person. you deserve to be warm."

the little girl started to get tense and scared.

"would you be open to me leaving the blankie in the middle and you can pick it up if you want it?"

the little girl smirked and shook her head yes.

"are you still open to me asking you another question?"

the little girl sat down and replied with a soft "yea."

"what would you like me to call you?"

the little girl put her head in her little hands as she slumped forward, "i don't know megs." she started to quietly weep.

"how about this, you think about it and tell me when you're ready, okay?"

the little girl looked up and shook her head yes.

"i'm going to turn around now, do you need anything else from me?

the little girl shook her head no.

"okay, you know where to find me. i'm not going anywhere."

megs put the blankie in the middle of the mountain top and turned around. the little girl ran to get the blankie then hurried and ran into her box and locked the door.

during phone time, i talked with julie, my high school math teacher. she was asking me about my recovery, and we talked about that for a while. she told me she was so glad i am getting help and how i scared her for a while. i told her that i think this time in treatment will be my last time in treatment. she told me that even if it's not my last time, it won't be as scary as this time. i really don't want to end up back in treatment though.

february 11, 2019

after i settled down for the day, my brain started processing things from my individual and family sessions.

as i was resting, i closed my eyes and was back at the top of the mountain. the little girl crawled out of her box and called for megs. megs turned around and said, "hi there." the little girl

was swaying back and forth with an excited smirk on her face as she looked at megs in awe.

"i know what i want you to call me now" the little girl told megs.

"oh really? what may that be?"

"i want you to call me honeybee."

the little girl couldn't control her excitement as she smiled and started jumping up and down.

during moon stories, i couldn't pay attention at all. i kept thinking of my family and individual session and how i couldn't protect my brudder. i started getting flashbacks of my dad and different events and close ups of his face when he would be raping me. i could hear him tell me "kiss me" and could feel his warm breath on my skin. i saw his eyes gently close as he enjoyed raping me then looking straight into his eyes as mine would start to water. i saw his mouth slightly open with his one crooked tooth in the front/side. i couldn't deal with the memories anymore so i forced myself to go back to sleep until i woke up sweating in fear.

i tried resting my eyes again and was brought back to the mountain top. honeybee was jumping with excitement. megs giggled with her soft voice, "you're very excited, i see." "yes" replied honeybee. all of sudden, honeybee stopped in her tracks and stared at megs with fear in her eyes. "what's wrong?" asked megs. "i need to go help my brudder. i need to save him." honeybee replied. honeybee ran into the dark, scary woods and came across a glowing branch. as she touched the branch, she was taken back in her childhood home.

i opened my eyes because i mentally couldn't process anymore.

february 13, 2019

addie keeps on increasing my meal plan and i'm freaking out.

during yoga i was brought back to the mountain top. scene. honeybee was in the woods in a memory with her brudder. honeybee got scared of the memories and started crying, hyperventilating, and freaking out. "megs!" honeybee screamed out in the little time she had in-between breaths. honeybee found a branch in her house that was glowing. as honeybee grabbed the branch, she was back in the woods running towards megs. honeybee stopped halfway between her cardboard box and kept looking between the two. back and forth. finally, honeybee dropped to the ground out of exhaustion. megs asked honeybee, "are you open to allowing me to help you calm down?" honeybee looked up through her watering eyes and gently nodded her head, yes. as a nonverbal cry/plead for help. "can you take three deep breaths for me?" honeybee took three deep breaths as she slowly stopped hyperventilating.
"there you go. what does the sky look like?"
"blue and grey mixed together with some clouds."
"what does the ground feel like?"
"it's hard and cold and bumpy."
"what can you hear?"
"i hear the birds chirping and water hitting the rocks."
"can you take a deep breath for me?"
honeybee inhales through her nose and exhales through her mouth.
"what do you smell?"
"i smell outside and a mountain smell."
"good job! how do you feel now?"
"i feel a wittle scared still but my heart isn't going up and down as fast."

"i'm glad you are feeling a little better. i know you must have been so scared."

honeybee nodded slowly. "can i go back in my box now? i'm sleepy."

"you can do whatever you would like. you have the choice and the control.

honeybee gave megs a little smirk and went into her box and shut the doors. this time though, honeybee did not lock them. megs turned around patiently waiting for honeybee to invite her again.

after group, addie pulled me for session. it was a good session. i love talking to her. she pushes me and shows me tough love. i can tell she truly cares about me. after i met with addie, lauren pulled me for my emdr session. she explained and showed me how emdr was going to go. we worked on creating a safe space. i chose my dance studio to turn to when i need to ground.

at night i was triggered and one of the techs was asking what was going on. i told her how my shower curtain has a space where it's clear and it was making me uncomfortable because growing up, my dad used to watch me shower. the tech went into a room that was not occupied and we switched the shower curtains.

february 18, 2019

while everyone was in yoga, i was working on my poster for the food and feelings group. addie came up to me after the staff's morning flash and sat on the ground with me. she told me she heard i had a rough weekend and that i wanted to leave. during the morning flash everyone was like "what do we do?" and addie said, "i'll go talk to her." so addie was talking to me for a little then showed me my new meal plan. i explained to her that when i was triggered, leaving was my first reaction but i know i need to be here. addie agreed and was very helpful. after addie talked to me, my therapist pulled me.

my therapist and i were talking about my triggers and how it's a habit for me to say "dad" when referring to my dad but i don't want to call him that anymore. i wanted to call him "j." i wanted to start calling him "j" because he doesn't earn the title of "dad" and i am just calling him that out of obligation. it was a really insightful session.

i woke up in the middle of the night and i am getting frustrated because i keep peeing a little in my sleep and i don't know why.

february 20, 2019

during yoga today i kept crying and it was getting to the point where i was starting to hyperventilate. i got up and walked out of group and lauren, the instructor, walked out behind me and told me to go to the nurse to let her know what's going on. i walked up to the nurse's station and was crying and hyperventilating. one of the techs walked out and was talking to me and i broke down and lost it. i am so tired and done with dealing with my past. i'm done reliving everything. i feel like i will never be able to get over it and it's always going to be affecting me. i am super anxious to be starting emdr. i'm having horrible body image. the more the trauma comes up, the more i want to engage in behaviors. i feel extremely defeated. i told the tech everything then one of the therapists, aubrey, came down the hall and asked if i needed support. the tech said yes because she didn't really know what to say. aubrey took me to her office and we talked some. she was like "this is only a chapter of your story, not the whole book." she was asking if i was suicidal and i told her no but if something were to happen to me, i wouldn't care.

after i was done talking with aubrey, it was time for my morning supplement and i told them i didn't want it. the nurse told me it was a part of my meal plan and i started crying. lof came up to me and supported me while i drank the supplement. lauren came to get me and asked if she wanted to have our session earlier. lauren grabbed me during food and feelings group and we had our session.

i told lauren what i've been struggling with she told me, "it's hard because i care about you but i have hope because this means you're healing, and your brain is healing. i don't like seeing you in pain though." we talked for a little and then got into the position for emdr. she asked me different questions and had me think of specific events. she wrote down one or two words or feelings so that we could go back to them. we focused on the earliest memory i could remember when i was three. i couldn't remember much but i could remember the body sensations.

i felt pain around my vagina and throughout my body. i kept having flashbacks of "j" fingering me and raping me in our house before the hurricane. i couldn't remember much. after we were done with the first emdr processing, i remembered literally every detail and now memories keep popping up. i am so mentally exhausted i can't even remember them all to write them down. the rest of the day i struggled to stay present. i didn't have snack. i barely had dinner. the memories were too much. emdr is hard. i kept refusing my supplements. i don't want to do this anymore. i became suicidal with a plan and intent. the nurse had me sleep in the day room the next couple of nights.

february 22, 2019

i started the harry potter series today. i've never read them
before. during yoga, lauren wasn't here today so another yoga
teacher led group.

*honeybee came out but she wasn't three anymore. she was four
or five. she brought her broken/damaged teddy bear and asked
megs if she could meet her in the middle. megs slowly walked
to the middle to meet honeybee. honeybee was still wearing her
dirty, pink nightgown. her hair was still tangled and her body
and face were still beaten and bruised. megs sat down criss
crossed with honeybee. it was sunny, but not too bright. birds
were chirping and there was a butterfly flying around. "thank
you for inviting me to come meet you. i know things have been
tough , huh?" honeybee replied, "yea, and scary." honeybee looked
up at megs with admiration. megs responded, "ya know, you're
a very resilient little one and i'm honored to get to know you."
honeybee sat in awe with her eyes glistening in the sun and gave
megs a little smirk.*
"can you fix one button on my teddy bear?"
"of course"
*as megs was gently sewing the button back on her teddy bear,
little bits of grass started growing through the cracks on the
mountain top. as megs was done, she handed honeybee back her
teddy bear and honeybee squeezed her bear tightly.*

after yoga was done i was so excited because all i could
think about was the growth happening. the fact honeybee
wasn't three anymore was a surprise to me because this week
i worked on memories from when i was three in emdr. i feel

like the grass growing and the teddy bear being fixed is a metaphor for healing.

march 1, 2019

i was back at the mountain top scene for a little bit and it was sunny. the box was closed and in that area, it was dark and scary. honeybee was standing up, smiling ever so slightly as she's skipping around in the grass that popped up. megs was sitting there smiling at her. honeybee grabbed megs's hand and pulled her up to spin with her. honeybee's bruises and cuts on her face were gone. she still had bruises and cuts on her arms and legs. her hair was still in knots and not brushed. she was still in her dirty, pink nightgown with holes in it. megs and honeybee's bond grew closer. megs is earning honeybee's trust and it is a beautiful thing to witness.

i told lauren about megs and honeybee skipping on the mountain top during our session and lauren offered for me to skip in real life. we skipped in her office and jumped up and down. it was amazing.

march 5, 2019

today is my family's commemoration day! growing up after "j" was taken away, one of my therapists suggested having a commemoration day. a day to celebrate and honor how far we have come as a family instead of dwelling on the anniversary "j" was taken away. every year on march 5, we do something special as a family to commemorate us. throughout treatment, i have decided that my dad does not earn the title of being called my dad and therefore, i started calling him by his first name. for safety reasons, he is going to be called "j" in this book.

i can't believe it has been nine years since "j" left. i really wish i could spend the day with my family but addie is trying to make today special for me. she let me pick out carrot cake! i have not had carrot cake in a hot sec. this year i feel happier and much more excited than previous years for commemoration day.

lof told me my skin is glowing today. that i was radiating happiness. that made me feel really good. i'm like, "hmmm could it be the nutrition?" lof replied with "yes. it is the nutrition." usually my "ed" would be fighting so hard but the "ed" was calm today. i feel like if i were to discharge soon i would be okay and be able to continue with recovery.

for lunch today we had restaurant outing and addie brought the carrot cake. she allowed it to be a challenge for anyone else who wanted to try it and celebrate with me. i was shocked at how so many people were excited to celebrate with me. the cake was really good. when we got back, lauren pulled me for my emdr session. it was a good session for the first time. i actually feel content and we even finished a memory. i feel disgusted at the act but i don't feel disgusted towards myself which is a huge step for me.

march 6, 2019

i met with some of treatment team today and they told me my discharge date is april 1!!!! i'm so excited but then i asked them if it was an april fool's day joke. addie laughed and told me she thought about that too. i feel motivated but i'm also terrified to be on my own after discharging.

i keep having really bad nightmares and vivid dreams about my abuse. lauren told me this is normal but i hate it. it's scary. i was talking to one of the nurses, aleisha, because she could tell i was having a rough day. we were talking and she says, "people are in our lives for a reason and they're either a blessin' or a lesson. i told her i push people away and it's going to be hard not to push people away before i discharge.

i came across a page in my journal designated to quotes addie would say. some of them still stick with me today. "my entire life is an affirmation" is my favorite. addie and i butt heads a few times but i love that i am able to be very blunt with her. she's honestly the first and only person i've ever been this blunt with—until i met my current therapist, catherine.

march 16, 2019

today i am going on my first pass alone. that means i get to leave the facility for a few hours and try to do recovery in "the real world" without the support of my peers and staff. during the morning group, i drew myself a permission slip to "give myself grace." i had everyone sign it. it felt good to have people supporting me on my outing and excited to see what i do.

when i went to leave, my car wouldn't start so aleisha had to jump start my car and i had to get my car fixed. what a way to start an outing. i was able to have my phone so i was calling and texting people the entire time trying to catch up. i went to ulta and got my hair cut. i felt like a new person. i went to the mall to go to aerie and got leggings and a top. i asked the girl that worked there her opinions on how it looked because my eating disorder was starting to act up because i was getting a different size than i wore before residential. after aerie, i went to build a bear. i was letting my inner child play and get what she wanted. that bear is super special to me.

on my way back to my treatment place, i facetimed with a friend. she told me i looked good and "gained the weight back." that sent my eating disorder on fire. when i hear that i look healthy etc. my eating disorder automatically goes to tell me that being healthy means i'm fat, etc.

in treatment we wrote a letter to ed. here is mine:

my dearest ed,

i want to start off by thanking you for serving a purpose in my life all of these years. thank you for protecting me and being a constant during the chaos. i am now learning new skills to help me cope—ones that won't harm me or kill me. i understand that was not your intention in the first place. you were trying to help. you wanted to give me control. at some point though, that shifted, and you became one of the things you were trying to protect me from. you still have a purpose in my life, i'm not getting rid of you completely. when you come into my life, i now know what i need to work on to better myself and utilize the skills i am learning to cope in a healthy way. i am not mad at you or scared of you anymore. i have found my sense of purpose, my worth. thank you for helping make me into the strong and resilient woman i am today. i am going to tuck you in bed with a cup of warm milk because i can handle life on my own right now.

love,
meghan.

When I first came to residential, I was so malnourished that I couldn't see how sick I was. I do not remember the first month of treatment because my brain was so foggy. The last days of residential, we continued EMDR which brought up a lot of memories. I struggled with my intake but kept moving forward. My mom and brudder came to visit me and go to a family day to learn about eating disorders and how to support me. I was allowed to have another pass to hang out with them. we went to the aquarium and to the mountains.

Mine and Addie's sessions became more about planning to discharge. My therapist pulled me into treatment team as a "goodbye." I walked into team and threw up my peace signs and sat down. Everyone was saying nice things to me and I cried. It was good to hear the nice things especially from the people I look up to. Addie's eyes were watering and she told me that she was really grateful she could be real with me and blunt. The director told me that I could make rapport with everyone I come in contact with. Aubrey told me how nice it was having me in group and how I stick up for my beliefs and values. Everyone told me they were honored to meet me.

Sometimes I wish I could see what others see in me. I can see glimpses sometimes when I'm in a motivated mood and feeling inspirational. On my last day of residential, all of the staff was so emotional saying bye to me. They've seen me at my lowest. They helped save my life. The staff at my treatment facility will forever hold a place in my heart.

The day after I discharged from residential, I started IOP. I felt motivated and was in the honeymoon phase for a few months. I went to a couple therapists because I couldn't find the right fit until I asked a therapist, Catherine, to work with me. I met Catherine in a trauma group that she led. I soon became close with the staff at my IOP center and my recovery journey continued.

I still think about what I learned from residential and my sessions with Addie. Going to residential honestly saved my life.

Journal prompt:

Use this page to draw yourself a permission slip for whatever you need. Grace? Forgiveness? Love? There are endless options! Be creative. Have others sign it if you want.

CHAPTER FOURTEEN:

my world is grey

When I got out of residential, I was thriving. I was in the "honeymoon" phase of treatment where I am extremely motivated and ready to take on the world. I started this book. I was genuinely happy. I was having all of my meals and my snacks. I was doing what I was supposed to do. I hung out with friends, tried pole dancing, I was thriving. Catherine and I decided it was a good time to continue trauma work. I was doing well. I was coping with the trauma in a healthy way and was painting again. soon the trauma started getting to me and the honeymoon phase was wearing off. i started missing snacks, slacking on meals, and exercising more. my weight was declining again but i was determined to stay out of residential. so, instead, i started sleeping around with guys.

sleeping around with guys was a way for me to numb out and feel like i was wanted. i felt important in the moment. i thought sleeping around was a coping tool until it started making the trauma flashbacks worse. i still did it though despite of being triggered. it was better than starving myself, right? that was my mindset. i couldn't see that i was still hurting myself.

around late august my boobs started leaking a milky dis-charged. i googled it and it said it was a sign of breast cancer. with having a family history of breast cancer i started getting a little concerned. i brushed it off though because i didn't want to deal with it—"i was fine." i mentioned the milky discharge to my friend sloan and she told me i was probably pregnant. i laughed and responded with no i'm not. i mean, how could i be pregnant? i was on birth control, used a condom, and was told by numerous doctors i couldn't become pregnant due to my trauma history. i brushed it off again. i had too many other things to worry about.

september third i went to have surgery to get my ton-sils taken out. the nurse did a routine pregnancy test after i changed into my gown and registered for the procedure. the nurse comes back and tells me that the pregnancy test was positive, and anesthesia will be in to cancel the procedure. i couldn't speak. this isn't real. i'm not pregnant. i haven't even missed my period yet. they need to take my tonsils out because i keep getting strep and it hurts. anesthesia comes in, tells me he cannot put me under due to the positive pregnancy test and tells me to follow up with my obgyn dr. hahahaha wuuuut.

i go to starbucks because it's super early and i wait for my obgyn dr's office to open. as soon as the office opens, i call them and i can't really talk because everything is coming out so fast.

"umm hi, i was supposed to get my tonsils out today but they said i'm pregnant so i can't and to follow up with you guys so i don't know what to do right now."

"okay, can you come in today for bloodwork?"

"yes!"

they got me an appointment and took blood work. i waited a few days and sure enough, i heard the words, "you are pregnant." they told me my hcg numbers and to go back in a few days to see if the numbers are going up. i came back in a few days and my numbers still continued to increase. they scheduled an ultrasound for the next week. i started getting sick to my stomach. was it from nerves? because i was pregnant? i can't keep this baby. i started looking through options of abortion and adoptions, talked with people, i was more conflicted than ever. i went to the ultrasound and saw the baby and as soon as i heard the heartbeat, i started crying. i started crying because the heartbeat is actually there, and the baby is alive. deep down i knew then that i could not have an abortion or give it up for adoption. my due date was may seventeenth. my biggest fear is my child growing up in an abusive home. if it is with me, i know that will not happen. i also knew i could not get an abortion for my own personal reasons.

i continued with my life and only let my close friends and therapist know until i was ten weeks pregnant. i figured people are going to start noticing especially because i started showing at eight weeks and have been throwing up nonstop since i became pregnant. i made an announcement and to my shock, people were extremely supportive. i was terrified thinking that because i was not married yet, people would shame me and be very discouraging. it was the complete opposite.

I continued going to the appointments and doing what I was supposed to do. Gaining weight from the pregnancy really messed with my eating disorder. My dietitian, Lisa, continued to support me and let me know I needed x amount of calories now that I was pregnant. The number terrified me but killing my child from not eating enough terrified me more. In October I was at a place where I was able to discharge from IOP.

I discharged and was doing great. I was still seeing Catherine and saw my outpatient dietitian (who i saw before residential). Months went by. I was still throwing up every day. As the months went by and my stomach grew, my body image became more and more of an issue. eating disorder thoughts flooded my mind. i was constantly keeping track of my weight at my ob appts and starting to restrict my food. i was lying again to my dietitian but she wasn't aware because i was still gaining weight from the pregnancy.

my therapist took action and suggested i step back up to iop. after fighting my whole treatment team for days i finally gave in. i was pissed at my therapist and cancelled our session and wrote her a long email. she responded with, "i'll keep your spot open." catherine puts up with my stubbornness and tells me what i don't want to hear. she's the best. i started back in iop and i felt like a failure. i've already been through this. i shouldn't have to be back. missy, one of the other therapists at iop, would tell me to give myself grace and remind me recovery isn't linear.

Around January, I finally came to terms that I was having this baby. I found out I was having a boy and decided to name him Greyson Russell. Russell after my maternal grandfather. My grandfather died from leukemia in 2017 and I was really close with him. I wish my grandpa could meet my son. One night I decided to rearrange my living room and when I moved the couch, I put myself into preterm labor at twenty-six weeks. I had to go to the hospital so the staff could give me shots to stop my labor. I was already a high-risk pregnancy because of my eating disorder history. The hospital staff got my contractions under control and I was able to go home. I continued to throw up every day until I gave birth to my son. My OB cleared me to fly to Florida to see my family and friends before the baby is due in May. I was able to stay with my aunt and she helped me eat and was there for me when my eating disorder thoughts became too much. She showered me with gifts for Greyson and I felt relaxed for the first time in I don't know how long. I didn't want to go back to Tennessee.

The end of March comes and I start going into preterm labor again. I was in and out of the hospital for days until my water broke. I was terrified. I called Sarah and told her my water broke and asked if she could take me to the hospital. She took me to the hospital and the entire time I kept apologizing for leaking in her car and telling her it's too early. Sarah calmed me down like she's done in the past and reassured me that everything was going to be okay. When I got to the hospital they still kept trying to stop my labor.

April second at 8:37am I welcomed a beautiful baby boy born at thirty-three weeks. I was able to hold him for a few seconds before they took him and put him on oxygen and transported him to the NICU at the local children's hospital. I cried as soon as they laid him on my bare stomach. I have never experienced so much love in my life. as the doctor was stitching my third degree tear up i felt empty. i no longer had my baby in my tummy and he was nowhere near me. the coronavirus was also going on so i was not allowed to have visitors. i ate some chicken nuggets and was brought to the postpartum room to recover. I was laying there constantly asking the nurse when i can go over to the NICU to see my son. Later that afternoon I got permission to go over to the NICU. when I saw my sweet boy, I was in awe. He was so little. I asked the nurse if I was allowed to hold him. She helped me get Grey out with all of his wires. I was terrified to hold him. He was so small. So fragile. I felt like I was going to break him. Grey and

I did kangaroo time for hours and I was so in love. Greyson was four pounds thirteen ounces and seventeen inches long.

i felt broken when i had to go back to the hospital where i was admitted. i should be with my son. i'm an awful mom. why do i have to leave him?! the nurse reminded me that i need to take care of myself and that i just gave birth. she was right. i was in a lot of pain and could barely walk. i tried sleeping but i was too concerned with what was going on with greyson.

When I was discharged from the hospital, I stayed in the NICU with Greyson until he was discharged. I slept on the couch. sometimes Sarah would bring me home to get things I needed then back to the hospital. I was exhausted, emotional, fatigued, and alone…so alone. I tried talking to people on the phone or through face-time but it wasn't the same. I cried a lot. Still had to attend IOP. Missed my therapy session before because I was so exhausted I slept through it. I missed Maslow. there was so much going on and I had no idea what I was doing.

Each milestone Greyson made, my heart filled with joy. The first time he was able to wear clothes because he started regulating his body temperature. When he passed his car seat test. When he got his IV taken out—a few less wires made all the difference. If you're a NICU parent, you understand. When he got his feeding tube out…I could go on and on. Even with all the progress there were still setbacks. Greyson wouldn't gain weight and even after the NICU, he had a hard time gaining weight.

After fifteen days in the NICU, we were able to go home. As i was driving away from the children's hospital, I looked in my rearview mirror and felt like I was in a dream. I was so excited to be out of the NICU with my baby and at the same time, extremely terrified. I am going home to no help. At the hospital I had all of the nurses. I don't know how to take care of a baby. So many 'what ifs' popped in my head.

Once i got home and settled in, it was like mothering my child was natural. i breast fed for a little but then i was not making enough. greyson wasn't gaining weight and when his doctor told me he's "failure to thrive" i felt like a failure and an awful mom. We got Greyson on a high calorie formula and he has been doing great ever since.

I never realized how hard being a single mom would be. I have gone so long without sleep I started hallucinating. I wouldn't change anything for the world though. Greyson has taught me patience. Love. Judgement. He is teaching me self-love. When my therapist brings Greyson up and asks if i would let Greyson do x,y,z, i would tell her "no. why are you bringing him into this?" Catherine would respond with "because you have better judgment for Greyson than you do for yourself." she's right. i have grown so much because of the little boy sleeping in his crib right now as i write this.

Greyson started getting a bunch of ear infections and had to have surgery to get tubes put in. he did great but had a really hard time coming off of the anesthesia. the fear i felt when he was having a hard time was awful. i felt helpless. i always tell catherine and missy that if anything ever happened to greyson i would end up back in residential.

grey has been the one person keeping me out of residential and continuing to better myself. my main motivation is that i want greyson to have a different childhood than what i had. he deserves it. he is innocent. as i'm watching greyson grow, i think to myself, "how could anyone do what my dad did to a child?"

Greyson is my world. He is my reason for breathing and getting up each day even when my eyes are as heavy as a five-ton truck. Even though all I want is to sleep in and have coffee and breakfast in bed. He is the reason I am working on finally being comfortable in my own skin. Even though I am a size bigger than I used to be, he relied on my body. He gave it purpose. For him, I will always love it. He is my reason I now know the importance of patience. Even though I sometimes miss the fast-paced life…even though I still get frustrated when I feel inefficient, Grey needs me to go at his pace. He is my priority right now. For him, I slow down. He is the reason I worry more than ever. Even though I know it won't change anything…even though I know it's not his fault, he is precious. He is vulnerable. For him, I will worry forever. He is the reason I am now filled with gratitude. Even though I get sad when things do not go my way…even though I sometimes lose sight of what I have, Grey is my constant reminder that I am blessed. He is the light at the end of every tunnel. For him, everything is worth it. He is the reason my heart is full. Even though i am grateful for my life before him, Grey has shown me a love like no other. He is remarkable. For him, my heart explodes.

He is my reason.

Greyson changed my life for the better.

I look back on the day he was born. Shaking and fearful, they handed me his fragile body. His tiny body so desperate to settle down against mine. To feel safe. For a moment, I remember the weight of this calling caught my breath. How could I ever be enough? I felt like so many other women who have started this journey before me knew so much. I am quieted as I came fully present to what was happening. Grey, still and contented on my stomach. I am humbled because I am all he wanted…and now I see, I am more than enough for him.

My miracle.

Write 10 things you are grateful for:

1.
_____

2.
_____

3.
_____

4.
_____

5.
_____

6.
_____

7.
_____

8.
_____

9.
_____

10.

_____

_____

CHAPTER FIFTEEN:

thriving. not just surviving.

While I was in residential, I made the decision I was going to change my last name because I didn't want to be tied to "j." On April 11, 2019, I went to the courts and changed my last name. One of the best decisions I made in my life. I changed my last name to my mom's maiden name, Huston, because I wanted to still be connected to my mom's side of the family. Changing my last name so it was not the same as two of my abusers was a big step in me thriving and not just surviving. I called Stacey from my treatment center in Florida and she told me it was like night and day talking to me. I asked to speak to Jenn and told her about my name change and she started crying. Having supportive people in my life is what helped me get this far.

Being a single mom is hard. If you're a single mom, I see you. When you are sitting in your room crying while your child is asleep because you feel like a bad parent, I see you. When you're so overwhelmed with stress and want to run away, I see you. When you haven't showered in days because you don't get a break, I see you.

Something I've learned throughout my recovery and being a mom is that showering, brushing my teeth, and taking care of myself become big wins. When I'm so depressed and can only get myself to take a shower, that's a huge win. When I eat while all I want to do is restrict, that's a huge win. Society likes to make us think that we're not doing enough. You're doing an amazing job. I'm doing an amazing job. We are each on our own journeys. There is no one way to live your life.

When Jenn told me there is more to surviving in life and that i could actually thrive, I didn't believe her. I'm here to tell you, I was wrong. There is so much more to life than just simply surviving. If you're in a place where surviving is all you can do right now. I see you. I understand. I've been there. Sometimes I am still there. It's okay you are where you are. I am here to tell you, life does get better. It may not seem like it, but it's true.

I still struggle with memories from my past. Depression. Anxiety. PTSD. Feeling like i'm not "good enough." What is different about me now than before is that I can now sit with those feelings and recognize them. I can work through those feelings with my therapist, Catherine, and my treatment team. I can talk to my best friend, Jenna, about them. I can text Missy , Andrea, or Stacey. The difference now is that I have a support system who cares about me enough to believe in me when I do not believe in myself. I encourage you to find people in your life who can do the same.

A few weeks ago, I was going through the drive thru at Sonic because I wanted a vanilla Dr. Pepper and when I got there I realized I was hungry. I ordered a corndog. I started freaking out because I already had my snack for the day and thought I was binging. I knew that wasn't true but that's what my eating disorder was telling me. I texted Missy and she reassured me and promised I wasn't binging. We talked through my thoughts and I told her I cried over a freaking corndog. I was trying to laugh at myself about it to cope like what was wrong with me? She responded with, "the distress is real honey. Girl, give yourself a break." She was right.

Grace.

I can allow myself to give other people grace and give them a break but when it comes to myself something stops me. She let me know that my healthy voice was coming in because I wasn't going to drink my supplement that is on my meal plan because I was "binging" but I reached out.

Growth.

I saw it. I acknowledged my eating disorder thoughts and moved on with my recovery. It's okay to need help. It's okay to reach out. We were not made to do this life on our own.

I started going to church again. I had a hard time with my faith and with God because I couldn't understand why everything that happened to me happened. It wasn't until I truly believed in free will. I was able to talk to some of my old college professors about my struggles with God. There are people out there willing to help. Something I had to learn to do is let people in.

I have been terrified of letting people in after "j" left because I didn't want to get hurt. It wasn't until I met my current treatment team where I let down my walls completely. Before this book was published, they were the only ones who knew my entire story beginning to end. I don't do this with everyone. It's important to find people you trust before you start letting walls down. I have fought my treatment team so hard and tried pushing them away and they have continued to be there for me without judgement. This is what helped build my trust.

Jenna and I started a podcast called, The Bees Knees, where we talk about our journeys with mental health. We talk about our experiences in life and let people know they're not alone. A podcast is something I've been wanting to do for a while but I've been held back by fear. I started thinking to myself, how long am I going to keep letting fear hold me back in life? I decided to go for it. Jenna and I got the equipment and recorded our first episode.

Growing up, I never thought I would be where I am today. I never thought I'd make it past age six. Age thirteen. Age twenty...here i am. Age twenty-three with a beautiful son, a beautiful life, and writing a book that i only hope can one day help someone else. Even if my story helps and touches just one person, everything was worth it.

I am not just surviving in my life. I am finally thriving.

Journal prompt:

Have a conversation with your inner child. Ask them what they need from you. Use your dominant hand when you are "talking" and your non dominant hand when your inner child is talking.

_____

_____

_____

_____

_____

_____

_____

_____

_____

_____

_____

_____

_____

YOU ARE WORTHY.

YOU ARE LOVED.

YOU ARE WANTED.

YOU ARE IMPORTANT.

YOU ARE KIND.

YOU ARE UNIQUE.

YOU ARE ALLOWED TO BE WHO EVER YOU
WANT TO BE...

MOST IMPORTANTLY, YOU ARE YOU.

AND THAT MY FRIEND WILL ALWAYS BE
GOOD ENOUGH.

CPSIA information can be obtained
at www.ICGtesting.com
Printed in the USA
BVHW081204290321
603635BV00003B/210